"The book every special needs family wishes they had years earlier—clear, hopeful, and grounded in lived experience."

–Carl Richards, *Author of Your Money*

"*Care, Protect, Grow* is the most comprehensive and compassionate guide for special needs families to financial and life planning I've ever read. The authors utilize their professional and lived experience to provide a step by step and easy to follow process filled with meaningful case studies. This book is so captivating, you don't want to put it down and I can't wait to share it with our community."

–Kari Luther Rosbeck, President and CEO, TSC Alliance

"*Care, Protect, Grow* is the bible for navigating care of a special needs child from diagnosis through adulthood. Regardless of where you are on this journey the book has something for everyone. Despite being a parent of a special needs adult as well as a health care professional, I learned new information and gems that I can incorporate into my plans for my son. These brave women share their stories, expertise and insights in all the areas of caring for children of all various special needs. It moves beyond traditional financial and estate planning and challenges parents to consider care needs in a comprehensive way, embrace advocacy, and navigate the complex government and legal landscape on behalf of their child now and into the future. All parents, grandparents and anyone who loves a child with disabilities can benefit from this easy-to-read manual."

–Susan Stacey, CEO, Providence Inland Northwest Hospital System

"Families like ours need guidance that feels human. *Care, Protect, Grow* offers a practical, compassionate roadmap for every family that's ready to plan, but doesn't know where to start."

–Amanda Lukof, Co-Founder & CEO, Eleplan Inc.

"As a physician who specialized in caring for children and youth with disabilities and chronic illnesses and the parent of individuals with disabilities, I have lived and seen the challenges of special needs planning from many perspectives. Not only can one not see the forests for trees, but more often one is so focused on day-to-day challenges that you can't see the tree for the bark. *Care, Protect, Grow* provides the framework to step back, reorient and work in a practical way to ensure that not only their challenged family member, but the entire family can create a better future for everyone."

–Dr. Harry Gewanter, Pediatric Rheumatologist, founder of Medical Home Plus, former President of the Medical Society of Virginia

"This book bridges the gap between expertise and empathy in a way our industry urgently needs. Kristin Carleton, Kathy Matthews, and Mary McDirmid offer families—and the professionals who serve them—a compassionate, research-informed roadmap for navigating caregiving and financial decision-making across generations. It is an empowering and deeply human contribution to the field."

–Lindsey Lewis, Managing Director and Chair, the American College Center for Women in Financial Services

"Informed, empowered, optimistic: These are three words that describe how I feel as the parent of a special needs child after reading this incredible book! The authors have created a uniquely powerful and comprehensive resource to promote not just financial security, but the holistic well-being of all family members. They have taken a topic which had previously filled me with dread and made me excited to get started planning! As both a mental health professional and a mom, I can't wait to recommend this book far and wide."

–Laura E. Knouse, Professor of Psychology, University of Richmond and Mom

"I am extremely pleased to endorse and advise parents to obtain and read the new book *Care, Protect, Grow*. This is the most complete guide devoted to this critical issue. Finally, competent and compassionate advice is available. I have worked with children, parents, and strategic scientists of teaching and behavior analysis for over 50 years in several countries. The advice provided in this book fills the longstanding gap in advice for parents."

–R. Douglas Greer, PhD., CABAS® SBA, SRS, Senior CABAS® Research Scientist, Foundation for the Advancement of a Strategic Science of Teaching, Professor Emeritus of Psychology and Education, Columbia University Teachers College and Graduate School of Arts and Sciences, Fellow of the Association for Behavior Analysis International

"As a financial planner and professor working in the financial planning field, including recent research on disability planning, I was genuinely grateful to read *Care Protect Grow: Empower Your Family through Special Needs Financial Planning*. The book is approachable, practical, and written with families in mind; it offers a thoughtful roadmap for planning a meaningful life when a loved one requires extra care. The Care, Protect, and Grow framework, combined with the authors' personal stories, makes this both a deeply human and highly useful resource. It is a resource I will recommend again and again."

–Inga Timmerman Ph.D., CFP®

CARE
PROTECT
GROW

CARE
PROTECT
GROW

Empower Your Family *through* Special Needs Financial Planning

KRISTIN CARLETON | KATHY MATTHEWS | MARY McDIRMID

WILEY

Copyright © 2026 by John Wiley & Sons, Inc. All rights reserved, including rights for text and data mining and training of artificial intelligence technologies or similar technologies.

Published by John Wiley & Sons, Inc., Hoboken, New Jersey.

No part of this publication may be reproduced, stored in a retrieval system, or transmitted in any form or by any means, electronic, mechanical, photocopying, recording, scanning, or otherwise, except as permitted under Section 107 or 108 of the 1976 United States Copyright Act, without either the prior written permission of the Publisher, or authorization through payment of the appropriate per-copy fee to the Copyright Clearance Center, Inc., 222 Rosewood Drive, Danvers, MA 01923, (978) 750-8400, fax (978) 750-4470, or on the web at www.copyright.com. Requests to the Publisher for permission should be addressed to the Permissions Department, John Wiley & Sons, Inc., 111 River Street, Hoboken, NJ 07030, (201) 748-6011, fax (201) 748-6008, or online at http://www.wiley.com/go/permission.

The manufacturer's authorized representative according to the EU General Product Safety Regulation is Wiley-VCH GmbH, Boschstr. 12, 69469 Weinheim, Germany, e-mail: Product_Safety@wiley.com.

Trademarks: Wiley and the Wiley logo are trademarks or registered trademarks of John Wiley & Sons, Inc. and/or its affiliates in the United States and other countries and may not be used without written permission. All other trademarks are the property of their respective owners. John Wiley & Sons, Inc. is not associated with any product or vendor mentioned in this book.

Limit of Liability/Disclaimer of Warranty: While the publisher and the authors have used their best efforts in preparing this work, including a review of the content of the work, neither the publisher nor the authors make any representations or warranties with respect to the accuracy or completeness of the contents of this work and specifically disclaim all warranties, including without limitation any implied warranties of merchantability or fitness for a particular purpose. Certain AI systems have been used in the creation of this work. No warranty may be created or extended by sales representatives, written sales materials or promotional statements for this work. The fact that an organization, website, or product is referred to in this work as a citation and/or potential source of further information does not mean that the publisher and authors endorse the information or services the organization, website, or product may provide or recommendations it may make. This work is sold with the understanding that the publisher is not engaged in rendering professional services. The advice and strategies contained herein may not be suitable for your situation. You should consult with a specialist where appropriate. Further, readers should be aware that websites listed in this work may have changed or disappeared between when this work was written and when it is read. Neither the publisher nor authors shall be liable for any loss of profit or any other commercial damages, including but not limited to special, incidental, consequential, or other damages.

Investment Advisory Services offered through Sound Income Strategies, LLC, an SEC Registered Investment Advisory Firm. All Needs Planning and Sound Income Strategies, LLC are not associated entities.

For general information on our other products and services or for technical support, please contact our Customer Care Department within the United States at (800) 762-2974, outside the United States at (317) 572-3993 or fax (317) 572-4002.

Wiley also publishes its books in a variety of electronic formats. Some content that appears in print may not be available in electronic formats. For more information about Wiley products, visit our web site at www.wiley.com.

Library of Congress Cataloging-in-Publication Data has been applied for:

Hardback ISBN: 9781394334667
ePDF ISBN: 9781394334681
ePub ISBN: 9781394334674

Cover Design: Wiley
Cover Image: © Mary Long/stock.adobe.com

Typesetting: Set in 11/14pt AvenirLTStd by Lumina Datamatics

This book is dedicated to our children: Rylee, Eli, Ethan, Andy, Ruth, and Charlie. You make our lives better, and we strive to leave this world a better place for you. Everything we do is to provide a path for you to the future you deserve.

Contents

Preface xi

Author's Statement on Publishing and AI Assistance xiii

Chapter 1	Introduction to Our Journeys	1
Chapter 2	Introduction to Special Needs Planning	9
Chapter 3	Advocacy Within the Planning Process	23
Chapter 4	Understanding and Building Your Care Plan	41
Chapter 5	Financial Planning Over Two Generations	63
Chapter 6	Government Benefits and Special Needs Planning	95
Chapter 7	Tax Flexibility and Strategy	119
Chapter 8	Insurance: Protecting the Future with Confidence	131
Chapter 9	Estate Planning Strategies and Concepts	147

Contents

Chapter 10	Special Needs Trusts: Their Role in Estate Planning	161
Chapter 11	Decision-making Support: Balancing Protection and Autonomy	175
Chapter 12	Investing for Two Lifetimes: Building Enduring Wealth Through Income and Growth	189
Chapter 13	Self-care: Preserving Your Health, Identity, and Well-being	203
Chapter 14	Relax and Enjoy	217
Chapter 15	Planning for Military Families	231
Chapter 16	Education, Section 504, IEPs, and Your Child	245
Chapter 17	Special Needs Planning and Grandparents	261
Chapter 18	Sibling Supports	271

Conclusion: The First Step Is Yours	283
Notes	287
Acknowledgments	291
About the Authors	293
Index	295

Preface

When the three of us—Kristin, Kathy, and Mary—first met, we each brought something deeply personal to the table: not just our professional experience as financial planners, professional advocates, licensed behavior analysts, and educators, but our lived experience as caregivers, advocates, and members of families who have navigated the complex world of disability supports. We came together with the shared mission of making planning for individuals with disabilities more accessible, more compassionate, and more effective.

Over the years, we have worked with hundreds of families. We've sat at kitchen tables and across Zoom screens, hearing the same questions again and again: Where do I start? What happens when I'm gone? How do I make sure my child is safe and supported—but also free to live the life they choose? How do I think about tomorrow when today is so difficult? How do I navigate this tangled web of supports, rules, laws, and systems? There are so many systems, and I am barely surviving.

We wrote this book because we wanted to offer families something more lasting than a consultation or a meeting. We wanted to create a guide—grounded in practical tools and compassionate stories—that could walk beside families as they make some of the most important decisions of their lives.

This book draws from our professional experiences as founders of All Needs Planning as well as our personal journeys. You'll see Kathy's background in education and lifelong service to individuals with disabilities, Mary's expertise in financial planning and insurance, and Kristin's financial, investment, and advocacy experience converge into the Care, Protect, Grow™ model throughout these pages. Together, we built a framework that honors the full complexity of planning across a lifetime—and across generations.

We also know that planning doesn't happen in a vacuum. Laws change. Benefits shift. The world keeps moving. But what doesn't change is the deep love that motivates families to plan—and the need for a clear, trusted guide.

Whether you're just starting out or refining an existing plan, our goal is to meet you where you are and walk alongside you. We hope this book gives you confidence, clarity, and community as you build a future that supports not just your loved one with a disability but every member of your family.

Thank you for letting us be part of your journey.

We are in this together,

Kristin, Kathy, and Mary
All Needs Planning

Author's Statement on Publishing and AI Assistance

This book is the original work of the authors: Kristin Carleton, Mary McDirmid, and Dr. Kathy Matthews—cofounders and partners at All Needs Planning. The ideas, voice, case studies, stories, and intellectual property within these pages reflect our professional expertise, lived experience, and years of collaboration with families navigating the complexities of special needs planning.

We acknowledge the use of artificial intelligence (AI) as a tool in the development of this manuscript. AI-assisted drafting was used to support clarity, enhance structure, format visual elements, and maintain consistency of tone. All content generated with AI was reviewed, edited, and finalized by the authors, with direct input and oversight throughout the writing process. Any facts, legal details, or professional recommendations were derived from our expertise and verified for accuracy.

The final manuscript represents the creative and intellectual efforts of the authors, supported by AI for editorial assistance only.

Author's Statement on Publishing and AI Assistance

AUTHOR'S PRIVACY NOTE

All family names have been changed to protect privacy. We have changed some details of stories as well to protect the identity and privacy of our clients. We know that many of our clients make up the most vulnerable of our population, and protecting their safety is our first priority.

Chapter 1

Introduction to Our Journeys

Every journey into special needs planning starts with a story. For most of us who work in this space, it isn't just a professional calling—it's personal. We each carry the lived experience of raising, caring for, or supporting someone with a disability. It's what drives us. It's what connects us. It's what inspired us to build something different.

The three of us—Kristin, Kathy, and Mary—came to special needs planning through our own unique and emotional paths. In sharing our stories, we hope to show you not only why we do this work, but how deeply we understand what you're going through. This book is about building a comprehensive plan that supports your loved one and your family across a lifetime. But first, we want to invite you into our lives and show you where this all began.

KRISTIN

My journey began the moment I received my son's diagnosis at 19 weeks pregnant.

Eli is my rainbow baby, born after two miscarriages. I had prayed so hard for him, and I went into the 19-week growth scan full of hope and excitement, ready to count fingers and toes. I remember being asked if I wanted a girl or a boy and responding, "I don't care, as long as it's healthy." What a statement, thinking back. The truth is I love him no matter what his health issues are; I am his mother no matter what.

That day obviously did not go as expected. The ultrasound tech kept returning to the same spot, then left the room and came back with a worried look. She told me to be sure to check my messages.

What followed was a blur of fear and uncertainty. My primary doctor was out of town, the midwife said she didn't have time to talk, and I was left with unanswered questions and growing panic. When I checked MyChart, I saw my first clue: thick nuchal folds. I was asked to come in for a blood test for Down syndrome. It came back negative—which didn't rule anything out and didn't ease my fear.

That was when I found out I was having a boy. I decided to celebrate him fully, regardless of what was coming. I booked a maternity shoot, bought bowties and suspenders, and leaned into the joy of this pregnancy. But the worry was always there. I was sent for an MRI at the children's hospital. The machine was loud. I was claustrophobic. The kind nurse offered me anxiety meds, which I declined—not knowing which was worse for my baby, my fear or the medication. The scan was quiet except for the clanging and the knowledge that my child's future was unknown.

That day, we received the diagnosis that changed everything. A developmental disability. No prognosis. No timeline. Just the vague words and the fear of the unknown. But I loved my son deeply and immediately, and I knew I would do everything I could to protect him.

I was already a financial planner by profession, and in my fear, I turned to what I knew best: planning. I searched for a path forward. I bought life insurance. I asked an attorney to draft a special needs trust (he gently told me to wait until Eli was born). I called early intervention. I joined a Facebook group for his brain disorder.

That group gave me my first true hope. It showed me that doctors don't know everything, and that the worst-case scenario doesn't always play out. I saw children smiling, riding bikes, going to school. I clung to that hope.

Over time, I realized that special needs planning is far more than a legal document and a letter of intent. Families need community, coordination, advocacy, and support. I searched for a service that tied it all together, and when I couldn't find it, I began to build it. I knew I wasn't alone, but I also knew the burden too often falls on parents to become experts in everything.

Here's the truth: disability affects everyone. One in ten children has a rare disease (see Figure 1.1).[1] One in five has a special healthcare need.[2] And according to the National Institutes of Health (NIH), families with a member who has a disability need 30% more income to achieve the same standard of living.[3] Planning for two lifetimes—your child's and your own—is essential.

My biggest "aha" moment? That this work boils down to a simple but powerful formula: **financial planning +**

Figure 1.1 Disability affects everyone.

individualized advocacy = better outcomes. We can't wait to show you how.

KATHY

My son Ethan is the reason I'm here today. But before Ethan, there was another chapter of my life.

I had spent nearly 20 years in the disability field, working in roles like teacher's assistant, special ed teacher, behavior analyst, and school director. I supported families, ran programs, and took pride in providing excellent care.

Then came Ethan.

His arrival was pure joy. I took countless pictures, posted everything on social media, and soaked in every moment. But as I returned to work and watched him grow, I began to see signs I had seen before—as a professional, not as a parent.

He loved spinning the tops of yogurt pouches. Running water mesmerized him more than any toy. When he passed from my arms to my mom's, he didn't look at her.

At just eight months, I knew: he had autism.

It was a strange dual role. By day I was a professional serving families like mine. By night I was a mom trying to hold it all together. I hoped things would get better, that maybe it was just a phase. But deep down, I knew.

When Ethan was seven, his brother Andy was born. Around the same time, our babysitter introduced me to Kristin Carleton. Kristin had organized a focus group to talk about special needs planning. I remember listening to her speak and feeling something shift. She wasn't just talking about the system—she was talking about building something better.

It was the first time I realized there might be another way. That maybe we didn't have to accept how hard it was. Maybe we could change it.

Kristin and I kept talking. As the world shut down during COVID-19, we started building something together. We merged her financial expertise with my clinical and advocacy background, and slowly, All Needs Planning came to life.

Today, I get to work with families and watch them move from chaos to clarity. I see the transformation happen, and it fills me with joy. I know we are doing something meaningful—not just for other families, but for mine too. And when I'm up late working, tired but determined, I remind myself: this is how we change the world.

MARY

Everything was going fine during the routine pregnancy ultrasound, until it wasn't. They found tumors on my daughter's heart. The doctor said it could be tuberous sclerosis.

I couldn't hear anything else after that. I just waited for her to stop talking so I could leave.

My mind was spinning. I had just lost my dad the month before, after a long fight with Parkinson's. Supporting him had been one of the hardest and most meaningful things I'd ever done. I took pride in my advocacy for him. I was his rock, and he was mine. And now, just weeks later, I was gearing up for another battle.

Ruth was born and spent 10 days in the Neonatal Intensive Care Unit (NICU). It was shorter than expected, but it was devastating to leave her behind when I went home. She had feeding issues, colic, and began having seizures at four months. I was a mom, a wife, a new employee at a new job, and I was scared. So, I did what I always do: I reached out. I asked for help.

In those early days, I didn't need a medical expert or a financial advisor. I needed a list of moms I could cry with. I needed someone who had been there.

I started networking. I met Holly, the executive director of a local nonprofit, and began learning and connecting. I helped organize a rare disease event in Spokane. I got involved. I wanted to learn everything at once and hold onto it—not keep relearning in crisis. I wanted to help others do the same.

And I wanted to enjoy my child.

We planned and advocated and made hard decisions. Ruth had neurosurgery in 2019. Since March 2020, she's been on a seizure vacation. This past summer, she went to a camp we never thought she'd attend. And we got to be her parents, not just her caregivers.

I pursued professional training. I became a chartered special needs consultant. I gave presentations. I found mentors. I connected with attorneys to streamline planning for families. I even led an office in Spokane for two years—but my heart kept pulling me back to special needs planning. That's where I belong.

Today, I strive for balance—between joy and sorrow, between protecting Ruth and letting her grow. I allow myself to feel what I feel, and I work on myself so I can keep showing up.

If I could go back, I'd tell myself, "be present." Feel the feelings. Get support. Learn to be curious with professionals. Build a team, not a power dynamic. Most of all, don't be afraid to raise your hand because someone *will* be there.

CLOSING THOUGHTS

These are our stories. Raw, imperfect, but real. They brought us together. They brought us here. And they shaped the planning model we now use every day to help other families find a path forward.

This is the beginning of the journey. We'll walk it with you.

Chapter 2

Introduction to Special Needs Planning

When we think of families preparing for a loved one with a disability, many imagine a clear path: finalize your legal documents/estate plan, maybe purchase life insurance, and you're done. But the truth is far more complex, deeply emotional, and different for every family.

The reality is that special needs planning should address the needs of the family by making sure that funding is available across all necessary lifetimes, protections are in place to protect those funding needs but also to protect vulnerable individuals from predatory behaviors and peoples, and provide support and opportunities for growth across the lifespan. We often work with families who have put documents in place but have not made sure that their values are reflected in their planning. Or families have addressed their values but did not realize that lack of planning in one area would put their child back on a waitlist for years for services they relied on daily.

CASE STUDY: THE SCHEFFLING FAMILY

Stephanie and James Scheffling have always been deeply committed parents. Their daughter, Jenny, a bright, social, and trusting 17-year-old with a rare chromosomal disorder, lights up every room she enters. She thrives at school, participates in Special Olympics basketball, and spends weekends hiking and painting with her parents. She adores her older brother James Jr., who's away at college but never forgets to call, send chocolates, or plan hiking trips when he's home.

Like many parents, Stephanie and James Sr. worked hard to do the "right" things. They established a standalone special needs trust with a respected elder law attorney and worked with a well-regarded retirement-focused financial advisor. They maximized their life and disability insurance coverage through their employers and followed sound advice.

But as Jenny neared adulthood, the cracks in the plan became visible.

Stephanie and James had never formally discussed with James Jr. what his future caregiving role might be, though there was a loose assumption he would eventually step in. Jenny's support needs were increasing, and finding reliable caregivers had become harder. Stephanie, an accounting firm partner, was exhausted, juggling work and caregiving, and missing the structure and reprieve of her office routine. James Sr., who ran a real estate business, worked long hours and hadn't formalized any succession or buyout plan with his junior partner. Their informal agreement seemed secure, but nothing was in writing.

Increasingly, the family found themselves staring down difficult questions. They realized they needed to start with writing down what supports they thought Jenny would need in adulthood, and then they could think about who will care for her. They had always believed James Jr. (Jenny's brother) would be her caregiver, but they were starting to realize that might be unrealistic. Since they struggled to run the family business and care for Jenny, if James Jr. also had a family of his own, how could he balance his own family, caring for Jenny, and running the family business? (And how could they make sure they really knew what James Jr. wanted, instead of just trying to live up to their expectations?)

They realized that they needed flexibility: to be able to leave the door open to James Jr. taking over the family business, but also allow themselves the ability to sell the business if that is the direction that they need to go either because James Jr. is not interested/capable, or because they need the additional funding to support them in retirement and provide for Jenny's lifetime.

Having a plan for their retirement meant facing the other elephant in the room: what about the third stage of their retirement, where they need care and can no longer provide care to Jenny themselves? Who will care for them, and who will care for Jenny? Putting all that on James Jr. seemed great when they weren't thinking through details; now that they had spent intentional time working through everything, they realized that it not only wasn't realistic, it also wasn't what they wanted for their son.

And then the final question—did they have enough money to leave for Jenny to support her needs through her lifetime?

In other words, would the inheritance they provide cover her lifetime cost of care?

They were discovering a truth many families face: that special needs planning isn't about checking boxes—it's about building a thoughtful, integrated roadmap for the whole family.

WHAT IS SPECIAL NEEDS PLANNING?

Special needs planning isn't only about planning for one individual. It must support the entire family. Every decision—from housing and retirement to medical care and work benefits—can have ripple effects. And while legal tools like trusts are essential, they're only one part of the process. Throughout this book we will provide information on the legal and other tools you need, as well as the framework and strategy your family will use to build a plan where everyone can thrive.

At All Needs Planning, we use a three-part approach that helps families go beyond the surface: Care → Protect → Grow. Let's explore together what this means.

Care: Start with Day-to-day Supports and Decisions

Care means identifying the needs of each family member—today and into the future. That includes financial management, therapy supports, government benefits, and daily caregiving roles. Identifying the daily decisions that need to be made, who is making those decisions, and who is doing the daily tasks and work is important. Some families are divided into a caregiver and a breadwinner—other families have two working parents who are dividing caregiving responsibilities between them. Still others have an additional family member—a grandparent, sibling, or extended family—who is providing additional supports. The first step to building the *Care* portion of your plan is understanding what you are actually doing today.

In Chapters 3 through 6, we will guide you through the *Care* portion of your Special Needs Plan: building a financial plan, a care plan, structuring and understanding the advocacy you are doing and what else is needed, and building your care plan. *Care* builds around what you have and are doing today and builds a framework to determine what you will need in the future. This is all done so that we can uncover any gaps or holes of what is and will be needed in the future.

The Schefflings began by focusing on their daily reality.

Some of the first questions they needed to ask revolved around Jenny's care. They needed to look at what supports she was receiving at school and in the home. They needed to take a deep dive into these supports and then think through their roles as caregivers. Stephanie and James were providing emotional, physical, and logistical support. And a lot of the logistical support involved not only transportation, but a complicated web of professionals that in a lot of ways was all in their head.

Of course, Jenny also had day-to-day needs. She had a routine that she relied on and had trouble when small changes arose. Her preferences and reactions and triggers had not been written down anywhere, which, as parents, is so common. We do not question or draw attention to the care we provide. We just do it.

And the last piece—it's not the most important piece, but it is the factor that most impacts longevity—is how much all this support costs. Not only what it costs today out of the parents' or caregivers' budget must be factored in, but also what it would actually cost for others to do it. Is it truly the work of one person? Or are the parents (as most of us are) wearing many different hats as they cared for Jenny? Thinking through what someone else would need to be paid through the many different hats is a crucial part of putting together a care plan.

Families should also assess benefits eligibility. They must look at all available benefits, such as Medicaid waivers/home and community-based service waivers (which will be covered in depth in Chapter 6), and understand what resources are available through those waivers, if they are eligible. Knowing how to implement those benefits is a huge part of special needs planning for many families.

There's also Social Security benefits and knowing where to start. From Supplemental Security Income (SSI, needs-based benefits) to Social Security and Social Security—Disabled Adult Child benefits (based on earnings records of either the individual or a wage-earning parent), these benefits will be covered in much more detail in Chapter 6 as well. While Medicaid waivers may provide funding directly for services; SSI and the DAC benefit may provide income to the individual—in this case, to Jenny. Knowing when and how these benefits come into play is an important part of the *Care* process within special needs planning.

The parents must look at what benefits are available to them and to their families as well. If either of them has access to employer benefits, these are a great source of what can be inexpensive benefits because they receive group pricing through their employer. From health and disability insurance to group term life insurance, these benefits may apply to the entire family. Combing through your employee benefits package and making sure you understand what is available, what would benefit your family, and the cost is worth the time and effort. Often these are the most cost-effective benefits available to you outside of government benefits.

Understanding which of those benefits can be transferred outside of the workplace and into retirement is crucial. Some group life insurance providers will offer the ability to convert the life insurance outside of the workplace. Other employers will offer the ability to keep your health insurance through your lifetime. Knowing which of these benefits can "port" outside your employment is a key component of your plan—and can save you thousands of dollars in the long run.

Pensions are another component of employee benefits that special needs families need to make sure they understand. If your family has access to an employer pension, be sure to read the pension section of Chapter 5 in its entirety. A survivor benefit pension plan could mean you don't have to purchase expensive permanent life insurance. Knowing the right questions to ask—and what your options are—is a key to your long-term success.

> **NOTE:** Don't be afraid to ask your Human Resources department for more information about policies. Sometimes, they might not have a current policy in place—but they may be willing to advocate on your behalf to make a change that will benefit your child. It never hurts to ask—the worst they could say is no!

With those questions addressed, the Schefflings were able to get a care plan in place for Jenny and to calculate her lifetime cost of care. They were able to assess their own budget, retirement income needs, and family balance sheets.

Going through this process forced them to sit down with each other and spend intentional time setting goals as a family and figuring out what was truly important to them. They realized that having a small cottage where they could vacation together—in the place where they knew Jenny would be comfortable, and they could spend time as a family—was at the top of their list. They also realized that staying in their home as long as they could, while also finding housing where Jenny was comfortable living without them, was a top priority.

Focusing on these goals helped them to realize what they would need financially to achieve them and to address their budget and investments accordingly. They did realize that purchasing a cottage—even a small one—in the small mountain resort town they had all come to love was going to put a dent in their retirement savings and leave a gap for Jenny's lifelong funding needs. They also realized that being paid for the family business—even if they ended up giving it to James Jr.—was going to be an important part of their plan. In other words, if he was going to take over the family business, they would still need to take some revenue from it in their retirement.

For the first time, they began to view their plan as one that spanned *two lifetimes*—theirs and Jenny's.

One crucial moment came when they realized Jenny's future relied heavily on public benefits. Like many middle-class families, they hadn't seen these programs as "for them." But through planning, they saw how Supplemental Security Income and Medicaid waiver programs[1] were essential in bridging their funding gap.

Jenny's eligibility for the **Disabled Adult Child (DAC) benefit** from Social Security (triggered when her parents retire and start collecting Social Security themselves, from their own working records and contributions to the system) became part of the retirement planning itself (more on this in Chapter 6).

And as they explored more, they also opened an **ABLE account**[2]—a tax-advantaged savings option that wouldn't jeopardize Jenny's benefits (more on this important tool in Chapter 5).

As you can see from the Schefflings, *Care* involves what you are doing today—and then adjusting to make sure you are using all available benefits, strategies, and supports—from all sources—that benefit you and your family. From employee benefits to tax-advantaged savings options, you owe it to yourself to make sure you are making the right daily decisions for your family—including making sure you know all the options available to you.

Ensuring that your family has a financial plan, care plan, and support/advocacy strategy set-up will make sure your family is cared for—now and into the future.

Protect: Legal Structures, Tax Efficiency, and Insurance Tools That Safeguard the Plan

After identifying their needs and goals, it was time to build protections around those insights. Too often, families start with a trust or will. But unless you've defined the support and financial structure first, those documents may not serve you well.

The Schefflings now approached legal planning with clarity. They were able to update their wills to name a successor and alternate guardian, naming James Jr. as successor, and their nephew as alternate. Their nephew was older than James (although not by much) and close with their family.

John was also excited to serve on the microboard (covered in Chapter 11). Their trustees were named, and they were able to instruct their trust on how to communicate with the microboard and make big decisions about Jenny's future and finances. Their attorney helped them develop a clear estate map that showed them how funds would flow. And they adjusted their business succession plan to include a structured buyout for James Sr.'s real estate business—a buyout that would be in place (although with a discount) even if it was James Jr. who purchased the business. A buy-sell insurance policy also made sure that if James Sr. dies, the company would have the money to buy out his family and/or hire someone else to run the business while keeping the business in the family's hands, thus further protecting Jenny and the family legacy.

By prioritizing *Care* before *Protect*, they could customize their legal tools, insurance vehicles, and tax efficiency with purpose.

The *Protect* portion of the model puts the guardrails on to make sure that every member of your family is protected. It protects your savings and makes sure that your family has the financial resources to be successful no matter what may go wrong. It provides legal instructions for your wishes for your family once you are no longer here and protects vulnerable family members from being taken advantage of by others. And last but not least, it maximizes your dollars so that fewer of them are paid to the IRS. In Chapters 7–11, we will discuss the different types of protections your family needs and how to navigate the different tools to make decisions for your family with confidence.

We find that the *Protect* portion is the part most families procrastinate on the most. They don't want to spend the money or put too much pressure on making the perfect and final decision. And YES—it is a big deal when you are choosing the team who will legally care for their loved one. Our best advice: don't risk your loved one's future because you're afraid that good enough isn't perfect—act today, making the best decision you can. Your decisions will be better than the government making the decisions for you—which is what you are relying on if you have no plan in place.

Grow: Moving Forward with Confidence

The *Grow* phase is about dreaming again. It's about setting long-term financial and personal goals—once survival is no longer the only priority. The reason we start with *Care* and then *Protect* is that if you first determine what you need, then you put in protections for what is needed. This frees up your capacity to help your family grow into the future you deserve.

For the Schefflings, this meant that they were able to refine their investments to support income over two generations. They were able to prioritize their own retirement—with James Sr. finally able to recognize that he would not have to work until he died—while also ensuring Jenny's future stability. James Jr. was involved in the family's decision-making, and finally able to voice that he really wanted to move to New York City and pursue his dream job of working on Wall Street. He wasn't giving up on the family business, but he wanted to try out a few other things first.

Jenny joined her microboard meetings. James Jr. felt freer knowing a plan was in place. Stephanie started reading for pleasure again. James Sr. played soccer with friends. They talked more—and feared the future less.

Why This Matters

Special needs planning is about relationships, structure, clarity, and follow-through. Research shows that most disability-related caregiving is done by family members—and the majority is unpaid.[3] According to the Family Caregiver Alliance, two out of five families are providing more than 40 hours a week of unpaid care to family members (see Figure 2.1).

Without a plan in place for how this care will continue, the fabric of your family is at risk—as well as the family member who relies on that care to survive. You may not have a family member available who has the capacity to put in more than 40 hours a week of unpaid labor—or a community who can step in to get it done on your behalf. Systems may not be in place to step in behind you. For most families, a primary caregiver is doing the majority of the care—and much of it they do without even consciously thinking about it. It's the "default parent" times 100. I have talked to many mothers who feel this is their duty and are happy to do it. Whatever your outlook on that is, planning for when you are not there to do the work is essential. Instead of planning, what we see often is parents/caregivers hoping and praying that they live longer than their child. It's heartbreaking—and avoidable.

2 out of 5 families
40+ Hours/Week
of Unpaid Labor

Figure 2.1 According to the Caregiver Alliance, two out of five families provide more than 40 hours a week of unpaid labor to a family member with a disability.

FINAL THOUGHTS

The sustainability of care depends on planning ahead, assembling a strong network, and ensuring every member of the family is supported. By using the Care, Protect, Grow model, you create a roadmap that evolves with you. We want you to know that you—yes, you and every member of your family—deserve a life defined by possibility, not by fear.

This is not just about legal documents or investment strategy. It's about honoring your loved one's life, protecting your peace of mind, and creating a path forward that reflects your values and dreams.

In the next chapter, we'll dig deeper into how advocacy is an important part of your plan—some you're probably doing without even thinking about it, and some where you might need additional direction.

Chapter 3

Advocacy Within the Planning Process

Every family with a loved one who has special needs has, in one way or another, become their advocate. We've had the privilege of witnessing extraordinary acts of advocacy—parents and caregivers who fight, day after day, to ensure their children can live full, meaningful lives.

Just yesterday, we spoke to a mother who filed a complaint with the Office of Civil Rights—eight years ago. Her son had been denied access to the high school's technology lab based solely on his diagnosis. No evaluation. No justification. He's since graduated, but she has kept the complaint alive, not for her son, but for the students who come after him. Eight years later, that advocacy continues to make a difference.

BUILDING SUSTAINABLE ADVOCACY

Advocacy doesn't always make headlines. Sometimes, it's in the quiet, everyday choices you make—like understanding your child's diagnosis, asking the right questions, or pushing for answers when none are offered. It can mean attending Individualized Education Program (IEP) meetings, challenging an unfair decision, or simply ensuring your child gets to experience joy, friendship, learning, and independence. Advocacy is often invisible to the outside world—but it is essential, nonetheless.

You may not even realize you're doing it anymore. It's become second nature—sitting through IEP meetings, stepping in when your child is mistreated at the park, waiting hours at the Social Security office to ensure your child receives essential benefits. You may have done all of this—or are just starting down this road. Regardless, you are already an advocate. And the truth is: you can't do it forever.

> **NOTE:** Advocacy is not a job title—it's a role we grow into. Often, it's invisible. But always, it's essential.

In its strongest form, advocacy doesn't just open doors—it funds the resources behind them. Many families believe they can personally finance their child's lifetime care. But the reality is often more complex. We encourage you to consult a professional for a long-term cost-of-care analysis. You might be surprised by what it reveals. Families often underestimate the value of their unpaid care and the true cost of replacing that support with paid services.

Most families need to supplement their caregiving with community, nonprofit, or government support—not just for financial reasons, but because some essential services are only available through public programs. For example, many group homes and day support programs only accept Medicaid waiver funding—private pay isn't even an option.

That's why advocacy is about more than fighting today's battles. It's about securing a system that supports your loved one now and into the future. One of the most vital tools for doing this is the Medicaid Home and Community-based Services (HCBS) waiver.

A BRIEF HISTORY OF DISABILITY RIGHTS ADVOCACY

To understand where we are today—and why advocacy remains vital—it helps to look back.

In the early twentieth century, individuals with disabilities were often institutionalized, isolated from society, and denied basic rights. It wasn't until the latter half of the century that grassroots activism began to challenge these norms. Parents were often at the forefront of this movement, advocating fiercely for their children's right to be educated, supported, and included in community life.

The following were key milestones in disability rights advocacy:

- 1975—The Education for All Handicapped Children Act (EAHCA): The precursor to IDEA, this law guaranteed access to public education for children with disabilities.
- 1990—The Americans with Disabilities Act (ADA): This landmark civil rights law prohibited discrimination and guaranteed equal opportunity in employment, transportation, and public accommodations.

- 1999—*Olmstead v. L.C.*: The Supreme Court ruled that individuals with disabilities have the right to receive services in the most integrated setting appropriate to their needs.

> **NOTE:** The disability rights movement has always been led by those most affected—families and individuals who refused to be invisible.

From forming early advocacy organizations to testifying before Congress, families have always played a crucial role. Many of today's laws and services were born from persistent, tireless family advocacy.

For example, a class action suit filed by parents of individuals with disabilities who were residents of Willowbrook State School in New York led to the Willowbrook Consent Judgment. More civil rights legislation followed the Consent Judgment, such as the Protection and Advocacy system in the Developmental Disabilities Assistance and Bill of Rights Act. Some believe the advocacy of parents, medical professionals, and importantly the reporting done by Geraldo Rivera around Willowbrook was the foundation of the disability advocacy movement in the United States.

Willowbrook is an example of what can happen when parents are uninformed and society does not value individuals with disabilities. Parents were encouraged to bring their kids to the institution, waitlists were long, and medical professionals often pushed for entry. Yet, the conditions inside were horrendous. One hundred percent of residents contracted hepatitis within six months. Fifty residents were cared for by one full-time staff and were left in their own feces, without access to proper sanitation or hygiene, food, medicine, education, support, or care.

Medical professionals working at Willowbrook brought in Geraldo Rivera in 1972 so he could film his famous expose, *Willowbrook: The Last Disgrace*. However, it was parent advocacy groups that filed the class action lawsuit that resulted the consent judgment mentioned previously and further civil rights legislation that benefits people with disabilities today.[1]

Much work has been done since—by self-advocates, advocates, families, and advocacy groups. But the work is far from over. Advocacy for people with disabilities continues to be important—especially as our society forgets the damage that institutions have done to people with disabilities and their families.

TEACHING SELF-ADVOCACY: BUILDING AUTONOMY THROUGH INCLUSION

While family-led advocacy is essential, one of the most transformative outcomes of advocacy is teaching individuals with disabilities to speak for themselves. Self-advocacy is not only a powerful act of personal empowerment—it's also a critical life skill that builds autonomy, strengthens decision-making capacity, and ensures that the individual's voice remains at the center of their own planning.

What Is Self-advocacy?

Self-advocacy means that a person with a disability is empowered and equipped to express their needs, make decisions about their life, and participate actively in planning their future. This doesn't happen overnight. It requires consistent support, modeling, and encouragement—from early childhood through adulthood.

Self-advocacy doesn't mean doing it all alone. It means having the tools, language, and confidence to participate meaningfully, even if the person needs assistance to do so. It also includes recognizing when to ask for help and how to communicate preferences in various settings—education, work, healthcare, housing, and social life.

Why It Matters

Far too often, people with disabilities are left out of conversations that directly impact them. Even with the best of intentions, families, professionals, and institutions may speak for the person rather than with them.

Person-centered planning flips that script. When we include the person with a disability in their own planning conversations—from IEP meetings to estate and care planning—we send a powerful message: "You matter. Your perspective matters. This plan is for you."

Teaching self-advocacy is a way to promote long-term independence. It reduces the risk of neglect, exploitation, or institutionalization. When people with disabilities know their rights and how to assert them, they are more likely to live safely and thrive in their communities.

HOW TO FOSTER SELF-ADVOCACY

Self-advocacy is a skill that needs to be started from a young age and practiced often. Starting with small decisions, honoring when a child lets you know their preferences is key. From picking clothes to choosing dinner and voicing preferences about routines, self-advocacy really starts with our ability to communicate.

You will notice that self-advocacy and decision-making overlap quite a bit. And they should: the ability to state your preferences is closely tied to your confidence in making decisions for yourself.

You will also note a key word here: communication. Speech therapy is getting a rebrand right now and becoming communication therapy—because we are noticing that many people with disabilities need alternate ways to communicate besides speech, such as AAC (augmentative and alternative communication) devices. Once a method of communication that works is figured out, self-advocacy and decision-making skills can be taught and developed. It seems simple, and these are skills we may take for granted, but the process can be lengthy and take intentional effort.

Modeling self-advocacy for yourself is an important part of this process as well. Noticing when your body is tired and allowing yourself to rest, or voicing the need for more physical space from someone who is causing you to feel crowded are important ways you can show your own self-advocacy. Make sure that your family has boundaries and respect them.

> **NOTE:** One of Kristin's favorite self-advocacy moments was when she took her kids to Disneyland, and both of them requested noise canceling headphones on a particularly noisy ride. Her son even requested that the headphones play his favorite calming meditation.

Supported decision-making can also help develop those advocacy muscles. Instead of making all decisions for the person without input from them, flip the script as they get older. Show your child a model where they can make their own decisions, after discussing and seeking feedback from you and/or others. While supported decision-making is more formally a model that can be used to support those with disabilities as adults, you can start this process at any time, with any type of decision.

Practicing how they can seek advice, frame a problem, and then analyze the consequences will be helpful toward their future. Breaking it down into visuals and/or appropriate language and taking as much time as they need to address the decision may be important—and worth it.

Looking into a more formal supported decision-making process in the future (discussed in more detail in Chapter 11) once your child turns 18 is an important part of the advocacy journey.

If you are starting to feel overwhelmed, take a step back. These are things you can incorporate into your daily routine and life without therapies or much additional time. As your child gets closer to age 18, working with their team to develop a more intentional plan around the path for their decision-making support and how highly developed their self-advocacy, communication, and decision-making skills is an important part of the transition to adulthood. That being said, self-advocacy is a skill that can be practiced over our lifetimes.

As the trusted adults/supportive voices to the individual with a disability, we have additional responsibilities as well. Creating safe practice spaces where we can roleplay the classroom, the doctor's/dentist's office, employment, and stores can be vitally important. Recognizing where issues are coming up—such as fear of asking to use the bathroom or of speaking up when someone is speaking too loudly for their comfort—and then helping roleplay those issues can help immensely.

And very generally, it is important to appreciate their likes and dislikes, comfort and discomfort and modeling for others how to do the same.

A recent conversation with a parent uncovered an example of this. She mentioned how her mother (grandmother of her son, who has autism) was brushing her son's hair. He was complaining, saying grandma was hurting him and to stop. She responded, "I'm not hurting you!" Mom came in at this part of the incident, and said to grandma, "Hey, you cannot tell him how his body feels. He said he's hurt; I need you to acknowledge that." While grandma had a hard time hearing this, the next time she brushed her grandson's hair, she asked him from the start to tell her how he preferred his hair brushed. She told him the objective was to get the knots out so he wouldn't need to chop off all his beautiful curls. And they worked together to get the hair brushing done—a beautiful story of teaching advocacy across generations.

Overall, teach your child their rights and responsibilities as they get older. Knowing both what is expected of them and what to expect of others and the systems around them will give them a better chance to advocate for themselves. And to say boldly—in whatever form of communication they "speak" with—I am important, I belong, and my needs are valid. And I respect your needs, importance, and belonging as well.

> **NOTE:** Don't wait until adulthood to teach advocacy. A five-year-old can learn to say, "I need a break." A teenager can learn to say, "This isn't working for me." If spoken words are not available to them, find alternate means of communication. The results are life changing.

PERSON-CENTERED PLANNING AND ADVOCACY

The goal of advocacy should never be to build a plan *for* someone—it should be to build a plan *with* them. This is the heart of person-centered planning. It requires us to listen deeply, remove assumptions, and honor the goals and dreams of the person with a disability.

In practical terms, this can be accomplished in many ways. Invite the individual to their own IEP or transition meetings. When a medical professional tries to have a conversation with only you about your child's health, be sure to include your child in the conversation. Explain what's happening in age-appropriate language that they can understand. And prepare them ahead of time if you will be discussing difficult behaviors, embarrassing items, or hard to talk about incidents.

Asking them open-ended questions can encourage them to start to figure out what they like and don't like. From food to TV shows to favorite outdoor activities, you might learn they have preferences you didn't even realize! Which can also allow you to provide what I call "real" choices—in other words, a choice where you are okay with whatever outcome they choose and will respect it. This looks different based on the age and capability of your child—but you might allow them to choose a morning activity, decide if they want to spend time with a relative, or decide what they want to eat for dinner. People with disabilities often crave structure and routine so much that we forget that they like and deserve to have choice and control over their surroundings as much as anyone else.

Self-advocacy also can be enacted in your legal planning. Invite your child to help choose who is on their microboard or care team. Make sure they are okay with the person you are planning to be their guardian in the future. The more you can involve them in the planning and communicate what the expectation is, the more likely a future transition will be smooth (or as smooth as possible).

A Legacy of Self-determination

When we teach and nurture self-advocacy, we are building more than independence—we are fostering self-determination. This is the ability to make choices, control one's own life, and live with dignity. It's what every person deserves, and it's what strong, sustainable advocacy supports.

> **NOTE:** If you're not at the table, you're on the menu. Self-advocacy makes sure people with disabilities take their rightful place at every table that matters.

When the individual becomes part of the advocacy team—when their voice is central and consistent—we move closer to a future where support systems are truly inclusive and autonomy is respected, not restricted.

One question we hear often is how self-advocacy can be fostered when a person has limited understanding, a tendency to self-harm, or is otherwise vulnerable. There are many daily decisions in one's life. When supporting an individual with decision-making, use the following guideposts in how to determine the best path forward.

Ask yourself if your reasoning for overriding their decision or not trusting their decision is more to do with their safety or about you wanting control. If it is about control, consider letting go and allowing them to make the decision. If it is truly about their safety, explain to them why you need to override it and that in the future, you will allow them to make other decisions. Consider finding another matter that they could exercise independence on: what to eat for breakfast or going to do a favorite activity.

When thinking about self-determination inside a group home, ask the question: can the individual make themselves a snack at any time of day or night if they are hungry? If the answer is no, start looking at every aspect of their day. Every person deserves some control over their lives. The ability to ask for (and make) a snack is one small example of how self-determination can (and should) be exercised in their everyday life.

While these examples are not all-inclusive, they help provide a framework for discussion with your support team.

The legal definition of competence will be explored in more depth in Chapter 11. Self-advocacy is not about legal competence. It's about an individual's ability to develop and express their preferences, needs, and wants. It's the center of person-centered planning.

The Work That Continues

While we've come a long way, families today still face immense challenges. There are long waitlists for Medicaid waivers, needed services/therapies/supports, and access to specialists. Public services are underfunded, and inclusive/special education is inconsistent and not available to everyone, especially those who live in rural areas. Housing options outside of the home are very limited for adults with disabilities.

In many cases, systems built to support individuals with disabilities are under strain—and families must step in to navigate or even supplement those supports.

We encourage you to consider taking action today. Join state-level advocacy coalitions. Many states have grassroots advocacy groups that push for policy change. Over the past 50 years, federal funding has become the backbone of many grassroots advocacy groups. With federal funding being reshaped, these groups may need to return to their roots—true grassroots advocacy driven by self-advocates, parents, and families. Now is the time to get involved and make sure your voice is heard.

Sharing your story is another wonderful form of advocacy. Stay within the bounds of what you are comfortable with. Showing up at city council meetings to share your story, PTA meetings, parent teacher conferences, social media, writing articles/blogs, and simply talking with other parents and friends can help show others the challenges still faced in the disability community. Personal narratives influence policymakers and public opinion.

Policy advocacy can be important as well. Contact your local, state, and national representatives. Ask for broader funding for waiver programs, education, and supported employment. Stay on top of the bills that are arriving in committee. Ask for meetings with representatives during the summer and talk about the challenges you're facing. If your state offers one, consider doing a Partners in Policymaking program.

And of course, share what you've learned. We have all found that other parents can be our best source of information. Learning from others who have actually walked the walk—and give real, lived experience advice—can be so helpful. Navigating systems can seem impossible, especially when many of the people who work to maintain the systems don't know the published rules themselves.

Often, localities have their own tips and tricks for how to navigate, what questions to ask, how to escalate, and what language to use. Other parents can help you find that out. Join Facebook groups, go to parent support groups, seek others out who are experiencing what you are.

And know this, as you advocate, as you seek change. *You are not alone.* It may feel like your child has a rare disease or more extreme behaviors or a unique set of challenges that others are not facing. All of those things may be true—*but yet,* disability forms a community of people who are there to listen, to seek to understand, and to help. There is a community of advocates, friends, and professionals waiting and wanting to help. We are in this together.

> **NOTE:** Advocacy is about systems change. When you fight for your child, you pave the way for someone else's too.

The advocacy landscape has evolved from exclusion to inclusion—but only through sustained effort. Your voice continues that tradition. Your story is the bridge to the future. We believe strongly that people with disabilities are human just like the rest of us. Their experiences, their voices, their contributions are needed and valued. This is why we value an inclusive society.

Advocacy comes in three major categories: the first is one's ability to express one's own preferences and advocate for your personal needs, the second is to know what one's rights are and to advocate to make sure that your rights are being respected and met, and the third is to change the systems in place to make sure your needs and those around you are being met.

We have talked quite a bit about self-advocacy. Now let's talk about how to make sure that your rights are being respected and met. In making sure your rights are respected and laws are being followed, you must know what those rights and laws are. You must know what the systems are that are available to you. And by reading this book, you are taking steps to make sure you are armed with this knowledge. Continue on this path—make sure your knowledge is current. Even as this book is being written, laws, policies, and systems are changing drastically. From the Secure Act to the One Big Beautiful Bill, to executive orders aimed at changing how federal agencies enact laws and distribute funding, systems are changing very quickly.

One example of how advocacy can directly impact your family is knowing about Social Security and the Medicaid waiver (covered in depth in Chapter 6). Being able to navigate those systems and obtain these benefits for your child—if they need them—can help secure not only medical benefits but housing, job supports, caregiver hours/personal care attendants, and small streams of income that can reduce the economic burden on parents who are caring for a child who is wholly dependent on them financially and otherwise. You will rarely see us use the word "burden" in this book—we do not think any human should ever be classified as a burden. In this context, the word is used to talk about the economic supports that we believe should be shared between families and the government in supporting someone with a disability.

Knowing the system is the first step. Learning how to navigate the system is the second. Then actually doing it—and staying on top of it—is advocacy that is such an important part of a special needs plan that it can mean the difference between success and failure. You should have confidence that your child will be cared for throughout their lifetime, knowing that you cannot do it on your own.

This part of advocacy is so important that when we founded our company, we made sure that we had a professional advocate on our ownership team who could guide us in creating plans for families—with advocacy front and center of the plan. Being able to obtain and coordinate all available resources is crucial to boosting the success of your plan.

And of course, if you have a school-aged child, you know the importance of advocacy in the education system. As we wrote this book, we intended for the IEP and advocacy to be a part of this chapter—but quickly realized that it deserved its own section. You can read all about IEPs in Chapter 19—a bonus chapter all about IEPs and navigating the education system.

The Individuals with Disabilities in Education Act (IDEA legislation) guarantees all students with disabilities access to a Free and Appropriate Public Education (you may have seen the acronym FAPE when referring to this). Knowing what protections Section 504 of the Rehabilitation Act of 1973 and the Americans with Disabilities Act of 1990 provide—and how that pertains to your child—is an important part of their rights and of your advocacy journey.

EMBEDDING ADVOCACY INTO YOUR PLAN

Advocacy is strongest when it's shared. Think beyond yourself—when appropriate, involve siblings, cousins, relatives, and friends. Consider creating a microboard—a small team of supporters who serve in a formalized setting to support your loved one with a disability. Document their preferences, routines, and red flags into a care plan. And in that care plan, outline the advocacy challenges you have had: issues you have worked through with their school, who those contacts are, what doctors have avoided providing needed care, etc.

Remember that advocacy can and should outlive you. It can be taught, documented, delegated, outsourced, and/or funded. When you put together your cost-of-care analysis in Chapter 5, remember advocacy as a key component that needs to be addressed. You may see advocacy as part of your (unpaid) job, but someone in the future may need to be paid to fulfill that role.

> **NOTE:** We don't advocate just for today. We advocate for the tomorrow we may never see.

Families often assume they can "just pay" for support, but that's rarely sustainable. One quick example is advocating for your child to receive the Medicaid waiver to cover their complex medical and caregiving needs. Following is an example of how much that would cost if the family were not providing it. We will go into more depth on these programs in Chapter 6, but the most important takeaway is not just how much it costs—but also that many of these programs *only accept individuals who are on state programs such as Medicaid waivers*. Many families are caught by surprise by this important fact—that even with millions of dollars, a self-pay option simply does not exist.

Medicaid Waiver Cost Snapshot

Service	Daily Cost	Monthly	Annual
In-home Support	$100	$3,000	$36,000
Day Program	$150	$4,500	$72,000
Residential Support	$300	$9,000	$108,000

State average reimbursement rates compiled by Kaiser Family Foundation: https://www.kff.org/.

As we mentioned earlier, advocacy falls into two main categories: first, educating yourself on what your child is entitled to and is available to them in the law and the community and making sure they are receiving what they need and want. The second category of advocacy is seeing where the law falls short and advocating for new laws and supports. Both these categories are critically important for the long-term success of both your family and the disability community as a whole. The majority of advocacy that we focus on in this book is in the first category, as we must build a plan around what currently exists. However, supports tend to grow and contract, and that is why planning must be flexible and change with what is happening in the world as well as in response to your family's needs.

FINAL THOUGHTS

You're already doing the hardest part—showing up, speaking up, and advocating daily. Our goal is to help you carry that load more sustainably and to show you how advocacy connects with every part of your financial, legal, and long-term planning.

Together, we'll build a system that doesn't rely on any one person but on a network that surrounds and supports your loved one. That's advocacy as a legacy.

You are not alone. And your voice—whether loud or quiet—is powerful. Let's build the future your child deserves. We are in this together.

Chapter 4

Understanding and Building Your Care Plan

Caregiving for a child with special needs is a profound commitment that requires emotional strength, practical skill, and unwavering resilience. Often families face a reality filled with daily demands, complex decisions, and ongoing advocacy. Without structured support, even the most devoted caregivers can become overwhelmed. To address these challenges, it is essential to develop structured, individualized care plans that empower both the child and their caregivers.

Although as caregivers, we "know" our child, often this knowledge is not shared with others in an intentional way. Sure, people around us may observe how we provide support, and some are maybe trained or knowledgeable in some ways. A **care plan** takes this a step further. It is a structured document containing detailed information about the person with a disability, their daily schedule, support needs, preferences, medications, important contacts, and so much more. Given how expert most caregivers are about the specific needs of their loved one, think about the care plan as the best-case-scenario way to quickly pass that knowledge onto someone else—and better yet, to use it to intentionally inform others of the needs, ahead of an urgent need.

A care plan is more than a document—it's a roadmap that outlines who is responsible for what, when, and how. It includes detailed information about medical conditions, educational goals, therapeutic interventions, emergency contacts, and long-term planning. For example, it might describe an IEP at school with weekly occupational therapy, consistent medication routines, and strategies for daily living at home.

> **NOTE:** We cheat a bit—and we encourage you to do the same. Instead of creating a separate letter of intent and care plan, we combine them into a single, unified document. Why? Because it saves time, energy, and confusion. Everything your child needs—daily routines, preferences, values, hopes, and plans—is in one place.

CASE STUDY: TERESA AND SARAH

Teresa carefully unfolds her daughter's fingers to help loosen the tight fist Sarah has been making. She gently massages Sarah's hand, using soothing words as she hits a point of tension. Sarah, who has severe spastic cerebral palsy, uses an AAC device to communicate, is in a wheelchair, and requires total assistance for all of her daily living activities. This stretching routine happens every hour, and though Sarah frowns when she's uncomfortable, she trusts Teresa implicitly.

During Sarah's school years, she had a one-on-one aide and consistent access to occupational therapy, a nurse, and an AAC device. Now 30, Sarah has aged out of school-based services. Teresa has become her full-time caregiver. Her routines—feeding, bathing, medication management, repositioning overnight—have become second nature. But no one else knows them like Teresa does.

The family's situation became even more complex when Teresa received an abnormal result from a mammogram. Suddenly, the question she had quietly feared for years became urgent: What will happen to Sarah if I can't care for her?

Teresa had never written down Sarah's daily needs—not because she didn't care, but because she was living them every day. But faced with her own health crisis, she and her husband Tomas knew it was time. They began building a care plan—not just for emergencies, but to provide clarity, comfort, and continuity for Sarah. Documenting things like Sarah's toileting routine, how she uses her communication device, what foods she enjoys, and how to transfer her safely became a powerful act of love.

As Sarah and Teresa collaborated on the plan, something beautiful happened: Sarah was able to voice her own preferences and even comfort her mom by building a playlist to support her during treatment. The act of planning empowered them both.

WHY CREATE A CARE PLAN?

Let's be honest—writing everything down can feel overwhelming. But that mental load you're carrying? That's exactly why a care plan is so valuable. By putting it all on paper (or digital file), you are fulfilling so many different purposes. Think of it as an act of love—you are making it easier for someone else to step in if needed—for the next caregiver and also for your loved one.

A good care plan clarifies what support your loved one actually receives (and still needs)—regardless of what stage of life they're in. We found when we put together our own care plans, this was one of the hardest parts—putting this down on paper, with no judgment to ourselves or our child on what their needs really are. And remember, this document is flexible, and you will want to update it! Your child will change and grow or regress over time—so the care plan should too.

Most importantly, the care plan lays the groundwork for long-term planning. It can support access to benefits and help you understand what services you will need to advocate for and help you prepare for emergency situations. If you have a "get out of dodge" pack—something you grab in case there is a fire—we recommend adding the care plan to it or saving it in a virtual space that is backed up appropriately. The care plan—while not a legal document—can serve as the foundation of future supports.

We have found that families end up using the care plan much more often than they originally thought they would. What started out as an exercise they were doing for a legal and legacy process, ends up being something that is useful in their everyday lives. A new babysitter, personal care attendant, independent living situation, and hospitalization—all are examples of how our families have used the care plan.

This is a great time to visit why we believe the care plan should be combined with the letter of intent. A traditional letter of intent is a very useful tool, but it falls short of a robust care plan. The letter of intent states what the family's desires are, their values, and the kind of life they want their loved one to live. It does not flesh out the day-to-day needs, risks, loves, and routines of your loved one. To us, a care plan encompasses both: the day-to-day needs as well as the overarching desires, wishes, and values of the family.

The care plan is an important part of the bigger picture. Care plans are not a standalone document. They're the first step in the planning process that includes advocacy and education (Chapters 3 and 15), government benefits (Chapter 6), financial and estate planning (Chapters 5 and 10), and microboards and support networks (Chapter 11).

When you pair a care plan with tools like a special needs trust, a microboard, and a team of dedicated professionals, you create a plan that is both personal and powerful. This document becomes your reference, your voice, and your guidepost—especially when you're not there to speak.

> **NOTE:** Think of your care plan as the backbone of your special needs plan. It's where real life meets strategy—and where love meets preparation.

CARE PLANS FOR INDEPENDENT BUT SUPPORTED ADULTS

Not every individual with a disability requires round-the-clock physical assistance. Many are capable of remarkable independence—and still need subtle but critical forms of support. These forms of "soft support"—monitoring, reminders, and planning—are just as essential as direct care. Care plans are equally important for these individuals, even if their needs aren't always visible.

Take Jason, for example. Jason is a 27-year-old man with autism who lives in a supported apartment and works part-time at the local library. From the outside, he appears highly independent—he takes the bus, cooks simple meals, and manages his work schedule. But Jason's independence is scaffolded by daily text reminders from his mom, visual calendars that help him track hygiene routines, and a job coach who checks in weekly.

Jason forgets to brush his teeth unless prompted and has difficulty planning meals for more than a couple of days at a time. He can shop for a few things at the grocery store but becomes overwhelmed by too many choices or unfamiliar layouts. A change in location of an item or section at the grocery store can send him into a tailspin. If a change in his work schedule happens unexpectedly, Jason often shuts down emotionally and skips his shift altogether. These are the kinds of details that may be missed without a care plan.

For individuals like Jason, the care plan may not include medical devices or toileting routines, but it should absolutely include the areas where Jason receives extra support that scaffold his independence. For Jason, that includes the frequency of reminders that his mom is giving, the time it's sent, the language that he is used to and responds well to, and what additional steps might need to be taken or ways to know that there is a problem happening. It goes beyond the detail of exactly what is happening and needed today and addresses the strategies and coping skills that Jason has (or lacks) and tools and tricks for addressing them effectively. It may include other professionals, motivations, and processes that have been brought in to address previous issues.

For example, Jason may have a favorite occupational therapist who is not needed regularly but is brought in when a new skill is needed. That person would be identified in the care plan, and the steps they use to teach Jason may be spelled out as well.

Here is a more in-depth example of how a small item, such as a text to remind Jason to brush his teeth, might become a large section of the care plan. Mom texts Jason every morning at 6:30 a.m. She knows that if she texts him at 7:30 a.m., he is too far along in his morning routine, and he takes it as a reprimand rather than a reminder. He becomes agitated and angry. Mom knows that if she misses this text, his entire day is disrupted, so she has actually set it to send out automatically from her phone so that she won't forget or sleep in by accident.

She also knows that Jason responds well to simple but direct language, while also reminding him that he is loved. They have their own special way of communicating—she reminds him that he has to fight the sugarbugs on his teeth and tells him he is loved and to have a great day. Jason usually responds with a picture of a bug—their own little inside joke. If he responds with words or emojis, she knows that something is off, and either calls him or stops by his apartment to check on him.

This is a small part of their routine, and one that they both take for granted and do without thinking. But these little details can be hugely helpful to someone else stepping in for his mom.

While these examples are specific to Jason, here are some categories to address in building your own care plan:

- A list of reminders needed for hygiene and health maintenance
- Strategies that help with executive functioning (e.g., time management, money skills)
- Communication strategies when overwhelmed or stressed

Figure 4.1 Making grocery shopping a successful experience.
Kevin Malik/Pexel

- Who to call when problems arise
- How to navigate transportation safely
- How to recognize signs that they're struggling

Thinking through the steps needed to go shopping can include how your loved one gets to the store, what support they need to navigate the store, what guidance they use when making shopping decisions, and all the other important steps involved in their experience (see Figure 4.1).

HOW TO CREATE A CARE PLAN

Creating a care plan for a more independent loved one is about preserving autonomy while ensuring safety. It gives support people—roommates, job coaches, extended family, or future caregivers—a clear picture of what makes this person successful, and what they still need.

> **NOTE:** Independence doesn't mean doing everything alone. It means having the right supports in place to succeed.

Start Small

We know how hard it can be to get started so first and foremost, start small. You don't have to do it all in one sitting. Pick one section per day. And use a template. We've created a downloadable, fillable template to guide you.

You can download our care plan template and customize it to meet your needs. As you get started, it can help to involve others. Don't do this alone. Include your spouse, your child (as appropriate), and other caregivers. And once you have it ready, make sure to review it annually. Update your plan regularly—ideally every year or after any major change.

Capture What You Know

We often hear from caregivers: "I know everything about my child—it's all in my head." And while that's true, putting it on paper can feel overwhelming. Here are some practical tips to help you start:

- Bring a notebook or open your phone's notes app. Carry it with you for a few days and jot down what you do without thinking. When do you offer reminders? When do you redirect behaviors? What do you prepare for in advance?
- Track your reminders. Every time you prompt your loved one to brush their teeth, take medicine, eat a snack, or

prepare for a change in routine—write it down. These are supports, even if they feel small.
- Observe transitions. Note how you help your child move from one activity to the next. Do you use a timer? A visual schedule? A favorite phrase or sensory tool? These details matter.
- Watch what you buy. Groceries, supplies, medications—your regular purchases can reveal hidden patterns and support needs. Are you avoiding certain foods or environments because of sensory issues? Are there favorite brands or tools your child relies on?
- Reflect on the "why." Ask yourself: "Why do I do this?" If you avoid certain situations or prep in specific ways, it's likely based on your child's needs. Write those insights down.
- Ask for help. Invite others to observe you or cowrite the care plan. Sometimes an outside perspective helps uncover routines you no longer notice.

This process doesn't have to be completed in one sitting. Choose one category at a time, and build your care plan gradually. Remember—you're not starting from scratch. You're simply capturing the incredible work you're already doing.

CONSIDERATIONS WHEN CREATING A CARE PLAN

As you upload the special knowledge you have of your loved one into your care plan, you may find that some of the support you have been providing is natural to you but may be difficult for others to understand. As parents and caregivers, we are immersed in the day to day. When we commit to writing our care plan, we are intentionally rising above the day to day and trying to communicate the support onto a document with the goal of helping others understand our loved one the way we do.

As we know, our loved ones may have specific support needs related to their nutrition, behavior, activities of daily living, routines, communication, and so much more. Let's dive into some of the different supports our loved ones may need and ways in which we meet those needs.

Describing How You Support Behaviors, Triggers, and Transitions

Behavior is a form of communication. Whether it's a meltdown in the grocery store, reluctance to meet someone new, or resistance during a doctor visit, behaviors often signal unmet needs, discomfort, or anxiety about upcoming changes. Including a behavior section in your care plan ensures that others can interpret and respond appropriately to your loved one's needs.

Everyone has triggers—sensory sensitivities, unexpected changes, loud noises, bright lights, or being touched without warning. For individuals with disabilities, especially those with autism or anxiety disorders, triggers can lead to shutdowns, outbursts, or withdrawal. If this pertains to your loved one, considering documenting triggering events such as (1) specific environments or situations that regularly cause stress (e.g., loud restaurants, long lines, crowded waiting rooms), (2) times of day when your child is more likely to become overwhelmed, (3) how sensory sensitivities show up (e.g., covering ears, avoiding eye contact, repetitive movements), and (4) preferred ways to self-regulate (e.g., noise-canceling headphones, fidget tools, access to a quiet space).

Describing Transitions

Whether it's moving from one activity to another or preparing for a major life event, transitions are a common challenge for many families. Here are some strategies you may be using that you could include in your care plan, but remember to include what works for *your* family and loved one, not simply what we suggest:

- **Visual schedules:** Help provide predictability. Include icons or photos if your child is nonreading.
- **Countdown timers:** Used to warn of upcoming transitions (e.g., "five more minutes").
- **Social stories:** Short illustrated narratives that describe what to expect in a new situation (meeting a doctor, visiting a new place).
- **Familiar routines:** Anchoring new transitions around familiar activities (e.g., always listening to a favorite song in the car before an appointment).
- **Transition objects:** Allowing your child to carry a familiar item during new experiences can provide emotional grounding.

Describing Supports That Are Needed to Handle Change

Some individuals with disabilities may find it challenging to meet new people, have a care provider change, or to go to an appointment. Think about your loved one and how you support this, which may include introducing new support staff or care providers gradually, ideally with you present; sending a brief introductory document about your loved one to new teachers, aides, or doctors before the first visit; requesting accommodations like extended appointment times or visits at less busy times; and using roleplay or videos to prep your child for upcoming interactions. Show pictures!

> **NOTE:** What looks like defiance or withdrawal is often fear, confusion, or sensory overload. Planning ahead isn't just helpful—it's compassionate.

By adding this section to your care plan, you're helping future caregivers, educators, or medical providers understand not just what your child needs—but how to support them in a way that respects their autonomy, comfort, and dignity.

Capturing the Fun Stuff: Joy, Interests, and Identity

One of the most beautiful and important parts of any care plan is highlighting the things that bring joy. While medical, behavioral, and logistical information is crucial, so too are the personal details that make your child uniquely who they are. This is where personality and happiness live.

These might seem like small things—but they matter a great deal. Including details about favorite activities, songs, TV shows, and leisure activities helps caregivers connect more authentically. It provides your loved one with comfort, continuity, and the opportunity to continue engaging in things they love—even if you are not the one facilitating them.

Consider including their favorite music or playlists (e.g., "Sarah loves The Eagles—especially 'Desperado'"); preferred sensory toys or fidgets (e.g., "Chews on a textured bracelet for calming"); favorite TV shows or movies (e.g., "Watches *Bluey* to relax before bedtime"); preferred colors, smells, and textures they enjoy; listing meaningful activities (e.g., "Attending inclusive yoga," "Reading graphic novels," "Going to the park every Sunday"); and sharing spiritual or cultural practices (e.g., "Loves lighting candles during Hanukkah," "Attends mass with grandma every Friday").

> **NOTE:** Fun is functional. What brings your child joy also brings connection, relaxation, and emotional well-being.

This section isn't fluff—it's foundational. When new caregivers know what lights your loved one up, they're more likely to connect meaningfully, creating comfort and consistency even in periods of change.

Example Care Plan

In addition to the foundational pieces, it helps to think through and document general information about your loved one to help provide more in-depth details. Table 4.1 breaks down all the sections of a care plan.

> **NOTE:** A care plan is not one-size-fits-all. It's a living, breathing document that evolves with your child. Start with what you know and build from there.

When the Unthinkable Happens

Teresa and Sarah's story is one example of what happens when a parent is suddenly unable to provide care. But it's not an anomaly—it's reality for thousands of families. A well-written care plan doesn't eliminate risk, but it softens the fall. It gives loved ones a roadmap and your child continuity of care.

Table 4.1 Step-by-step Care Plan

Start by describing your loved one's personality, strengths, likes, and aspirations.	The introduction gives the reader a snapshot of your loved one's current status. It describes who they are, their age, where they live, what they generally like to do, and anything that is currently underway. For example, Sam is 22 years old and in his own apartment in his family's home. He just graduated from high school and is attending a local day support program with other adults with autism. He enjoys going out into the community, especially volunteering at the Children's Museum, while at his day support program. At home, he helps his parents by taking the trash out and vacuuming the living room. When he isn't at his day program or helping out at home, he likes to watch YouTube videos on his iPad in his apartment.
Describe their diagnoses, medications, doctors, allergies, treatment history.	This section is best arranged as a list showing your loved one's medication, diagnosis (or reason for the medicine), schedule, and prescribing doctor. This section may also include a list of allergies or other treatments alongside information about the doctor or provider and frequency.
Medication, Reason, Schedule, Prescribing Doctor, Other Details	Guanfacine, ADHD, daily at night, Dr. Gould, Appointment with doctor every three months to review

(Continued)

Table 4.1 (Continued)

Provide information on their typical schedule, transitions, sensory or behavioral notes.	A daily routine can be described as well as listed in a table format to show the reader to illustrate daily events and support needs. It might show the time your loved one wakes up (and whether they wake on their own or need help), it may show where they go in the mornings (and describe if they need to take a lunch or other belongings with them), it may describe how they get to where they are going, what they do when they get there, when they return back home, and all the way into the night time routine. Providing a daily routine helps to share what a "day in the life" looks like and where support is needed. It can also easily be turned into a checklist to help someone who is stepping in to provide care to keep track of what is happening and when to support.
Explain how your loved one communicates, preferred language or tools (e.g., AAC).	Describing communication preferences and support needs is essential. Sometimes we have a familiar way in which we communicate with our loved one that is harder for others to relate to. It can help to describe this and to provide helpful tips. For example, Sally uses some vocal approximations when communicating, such as saying "h" for "hi" when greeting someone. But, if you remind her to use her AAC device, she can engage much more easily.

Describe any dietary needs, allergies, feeding routines, preferences.	This section should detail meal times, preferences, and support needs. If your loved one prepares their own meals, describe that. If you (or someone else) provides meals, explain that and offer insight into what types of meals. It is also important to describe the meal schedule. What time of day is best for meals? What about snacks? Are there any dietary restrictions or allergies? Sometimes it helps to provide pictures or specific details; try to remember that the person reading the care plan may not have any familiarity with the level of care you have grown so accustomed to.
Describe the level of support needed, routines, behavioral accommodations.	Toileting and hygiene routines are specific topics here as some individuals need detailed help or supports in these areas. These are also areas where we want to be sure to honor preferences and maintain the dignity of the person we are supporting. Use this section to describe what your loved one's current routines are and how you effectively support their needs. As with Jason earlier, he needs a daily reminder to brush his teeth, and that reminder must be timely. Let's use another example: Rob needs full assistance for toileting. When he wakes in the morning, his dad pushes his wheelchair into the bathroom and fully assists Rob to remove his overnight incontinence brief, fully assists in cleaning Rob and ensuring his skin is dry, and then places a new incontinence brief on, before putting a fresh set of clothes on him. We could further explain this to say that all of Rob's hygiene items are kept in the bathroom closet and that is it important to take a fresh pair of clothes in there with you before starting the routine.

(Continued)

Table 4.1 (Continued)

Provide information on your loved one's routine, safety concerns, overnight care or monitoring.	In this section, we want to make sure to document details around the sleeping routine. What time is bedtime? What activities lead up to bedtime (such as taking a bath beforehand)? Be sure to document safety concerns. For example, perhaps you are not actively monitoring your loved one while they sleep but you are aware if they wake. Meaning it could be important to say, "Michael sleeps in his bed on his own with his door closed, but sometimes he wakes during the night to go to the bathroom. If he does, we listen to make sure he goes back to bed on his own. If he doesn't go back to his bed and seems to be making his way down to the kitchen, we get up and redirect him back to his bed. Once we do that, he typically sleeps until morning." Those kinds of details are the kinds that we as parents might overlook because they seem so natural. But a new caregiver wouldn't know unless we told them. These are the kind of details you need in your care plan.
Describe known triggers, strategies that help, comfort items.	In addition to what is covered in this chapter on managing behaviors, make sure to list those details here in the care plan, paying special attention to how to address them so that the novice caregiver can have a better chance at addressing your loved one's needs in a way that has a history of success.

Share their favorite activities, relationships, and community involvement.	It helps tremendously to take time to note what your loved one likes to do. This can include where they typically go, such as attending events at your church or a local nonprofit, participating in Special Olympics, or visiting a sibling on the weekend. It can also list activities that they like to do such as walking in the neighborhood, getting ice cream from the local shop, and swimming in the neighborhood pool in the summers. Describing the activity, frequency, and support needed for that activity is important.
Provide information and copies of their IEP, transition goals, job programs, and vocational supports.	Chapter 16 is fully dedicated to understanding IEPs and transition planning, which includes employment. But here in this section of your care plan, what you are doing is noting what type of program your loved one is in, how often they go, how they get there, and what support is needed. For example, Jude goes to a private school called Northrun; he has an IEP that provides academic, behavioral, and social supports; and he attends a vocational class within that program where he interns at the local veterinarian's office once a week.

(Continued)

Table 4.1 *(Continued)*

Describe their routines, adaptations, eligibility for paratransit, and known routes.	Your loved one's care plan should detail your loved one's support need for transportation. Perhaps they take an Uber-type of service but need help using the app. Or perhaps they take the bus but need someone to take time with them to review the schedule and plan. Or maybe they drive on their own but need assistance when it rains or if there is a road change. Or maybe you are providing transportation and note the time to leave and pick up, including specifics on the location and how you communicate with your loved one when you arrive for pick up.
Identify key people to call, roles, and backup caregivers.	Emergency contacts are critical. We want to use this section to capture the names, relationship, and contact information for individuals who can be contacted. These might be family members, neighbors, case managers, anyone you can think of that would be important to know and reach out to, if needed.
Describe what your loved one wants for their future—home, relationships, and independence.	This section is last, but not least at all. It helps tremendously to identify your loved one's personal goals. Letting the reader know what your loved one is aspiring to do, what they are seeking in terms of relationships, or their home life can be very helpful. Take time here to note their goals and dreams, which will help those around them in their ongoing encouragement and support of them.

FINAL THOUGHTS

Your care plan won't just help others care for your loved one. It will help your loved one thrive, no matter who is by their side. You are the expert on your child. Let's get your expertise on paper.

Chapter 5

Financial Planning Over Two Generations

If you're caring for someone with a disability, you already know what it means to think ahead. You've likely thought about next week's appointments, next month's school IEP, and next year's service eligibility. But special needs planning stretches further. It spans decades—yours and theirs. Financial planning in this context isn't about your retirement *or* your child's needs. It's about both. A plan that truly works must sustain two generations.

Too often, families believe they can compartmentalize. "I'll plan for my retirement, and the kids will work themselves out." Or the opposite—I'll work until I'm dead so that my child is cared for, but I won't save anything for myself or plan for our needs. But for caregivers of children with lifelong needs, that thinking doesn't hold up. What happens to your child when you're no longer around? Who will step in—not just emotionally or logistically, but financially? Who will care for you—and your child—when you need care and your child does too? We will dive into how caregivers can prepare not only for their own retirement but for the economic well-being of their disabled child's lifetime as well.

Traditional financial plans often stop at retirement. Ours sees retirement as the first stop—and continues for the lifetime of our loved ones.

Families don't set out to create gaps in their planning, but without proper guidance, that's exactly what happens. We've seen families save diligently, only to have funds run out far earlier than expected. We've seen inheritances mismanaged, benefits lost due to improper account titling, and loved ones placed in settings that don't meet their needs—all preventable with a bit of proactive work.

That's why we believe in creating a multigenerational financial plan—a blueprint that balances your own well-being with your child's lifelong support. In this chapter, we'll show you how to calculate a realistic cost of care for your loved one. We will walk you through how to fund both your retirement and your child's future—while identifying the right tools to make sure that happens. We will walk you through tools such as ABLE accounts, different types of savings accounts, and how to identify gaps in your financial plan. And we will show you how to quantify what government benefits can pay for, and how personal savings can pair with government benefits to provide a lifetime of funding and having your child's needs met.

You will notice that the big theme of special needs planning is that everything works together. When you answer one question, five others come up. It can be difficult to isolate one topic—but in this chapter, we will do our best to show you how at its core, financial planning for your special needs family helps you isolate your needs heading into retirement, different from the lifelong needs of your child—and how your planning needs to encapsulate both.

And yes, we'll walk you through the tough questions too: What happens if your child outlives you by 30, 40, or even 50 years? What happens if you run out of money before they do?

These are heavy questions. But the right plan brings peace of mind, clarity, and control. And you don't have to do it alone.

> **NOTE:** A good plan gives your loved one a future. A great plan gives you the confidence to enjoy today.

CASE STUDY: LEARNING THE HARD WAY

Let's take a look at one family's journey to show how important multigenerational financial planning really is.

Jeb is a 48-year-old man with Down syndrome. For his entire life, he lived with his father, Jacob, in a stable and predictable home. They had a routine: coffee together at 5 a.m., checking the calendar, and reading the paper. Jeb thrived on that structure.

Jacob, well-intentioned and careful, set up a special needs trust for Jeb and saved diligently—leaving more than $2 million. He appointed a trusted cousin, Debbie, as trustee, but didn't fully prepare her for the role. Nor did he educate his daughters, Janice and Jeanine, who had promised to help with Jeb's care but were unaware of the trust's structure.

After Jacob's death, the money transferred properly, but the planning gaps quickly became clear. Jeb was moved into an assisted living facility, where his needs weren't fully met. Debbie, doing her best, hired extra caregivers and began spending down the trust for daily living expenses, unaware that other options—like Medicaid waivers—might be available.

Five years later, after market losses and escalating care costs, the trust had lost more than half its value. A cost-of-care analysis revealed that Jeb's funds wouldn't last another 15 years—let alone the 40 years he was expected to live. Debbie sought help, and only then learned about Medicaid benefits and additional supports that could have preserved the trust.

Through professional guidance, they adjusted course. Jeb qualified for a Medicaid waiver and moved into a more supportive group setting. A visual calendar helped recreate the structure he once had with his father. A therapist helped him work through grief. The trust was now used for extras—not essentials—and Jeb's quality of life dramatically improved.

While Jeb's father looked forward to the next generation, by not understanding what Jeb's costs would be without him there, and not using the right tools, his plan was incomplete, and his dollars did not stretch as far as needed.

This is a cautionary tale, not a failure. Jacob did the best he could with the information he had. But with more complete guidance, his $2 million could have supported Jeb for the rest of his life.

> **NOTE:** Good intentions need great planning. Trusts, benefits, and budgeting must work together to last a lifetime.

COST OF CARE: HOW TO ESTIMATE THE REAL NUMBERS

Special needs financial planning begins with understanding what your child's care will actually cost over their lifetime. That starts with a "cost-of-care" estimate. You will want to look at direct and indirect expenses—both what you are actually paying for as well as support that you provide but are not paid for.

Let's start with the tangible expenses. We recommend separating these out into categories: direct expenses, support services, medical costs, recreation and socialization, and oversight and management. Direct expenses include things like housing, food, clothing, and transportation. Don't forget to include maintenance for a home or car, Uber fees if used, and utilities.

Support services will include personal care aides, coaches, vocational support, and out-of-pocket therapies. Medical expenses are fairly obvious, with one caveat—think through if you want to have money set aside for therapies or treatments that may become available in the future but are not covered by insurance. We are seeing the trend is for health insurance companies to deny all treatments that they deem unnecessary—and their definition of unnecessary may not coincide with yours.

Remember in these expenses that you're tracking things that are not covered by Medicaid or their health insurance—as long as that health insurance will still be available to them throughout their lifetime. But don't include your company health insurance if your child is 20 and will get kicked off your company's health insurance at age 26.

Of course, recreation and socialization are also important. One family we know sends their adult son with Down syndrome on a special trip every year. He travels with other friends who have Down syndrome, there is a paid chaperone, he is escorted through the airport—and it is his absolute favorite part of the year. He talks about it constantly, hangs pictures on his wall in his bedroom at the group home he lives in, and has a countdown calendar. Participation in the Special Olympics, special memberships (think gaming or other online memberships), and camps are other examples to think of. These are not comprehensive examples of course—we provide these to help jog your memory of what may be applicable to your child and your family.

Another example of tangible expenses are professional services needed. A care manager, professional advocate, trustee, professional guardian. If you are not here, will these services be needed? And if they are needed, think through if the person providing them will need to be compensated.

Example: The Real Cost of Care

Let's walk through an example together. These numbers are loosely based on a client of ours who did not have the Medicaid waiver when we first met them. Their son was living in a group home that the family was paying for. It's important to note that while some group homes will accept private pay, many will not—many are set-up to only accept Medicaid waiver payments, as they see private pay as too risky for their business model.

The average monthly cost of a group home is $6,500, according to the Department of Medical Assistance Services (DMAS—Virginia Medicaid),[1] and varies depending on the level of support one needs and any other services they may be receiving. This family's son—let's call him Will—was in a middle tier support group home but was having some significant behavioral issues. The family started paying out of pocket for a personal care attendant to come and take Will out on activities to help reduce his behaviors.

What they thought would be a short-term support lasted three years—and showed no sign of going away. He also went on an annual beach trip with his family that cost $2,000 for his share, spent about $3,000 annually on gaming, and they had engaged a coach to see if they could get him working again—an activity he had really enjoyed when he first graduated high school.

Fleshing those expenses out, here are the numbers:

- Group Home: $90,000/year
- Personal Care Aide (part-time): $36,000/year
- Recreation and Social Activities: $5,000/year
- Job Coaching: $4,000/year
- **Total Annual Cost:** $135,000/year

Now multiply by life expectancy—and factor in inflation. Will was in his 30s at the time, and his lifelong cost of care was close to $5 million.

> **NOTE:** Knowing the number is the first step to building a plan. For a free downloadable cost-of-care template, visit: www.allneedsplanning.com/template/costofcare and enter code **FAMILYFIRST**.

PLANNING FOR YOUR RETIREMENT, FIRST

In special needs financial planning, it's common—too common, actually—for parents to focus entirely on their child's future while ignoring their own. We get it. When you love someone with a disability, the thought of something happening to *you* often feels secondary to making sure *they'll* be okay. We hear often that parents say—we have to work forever, and we have to outlive our child. But the reality is that in many cases, that is not going to happen.

And here's the truth: your retirement isn't just about you. It's about them too. If your own financial foundation crumbles—if you run out of money in your 70s or 80s—it's your loved one who may feel the consequences. Without planning, you may find yourself pulling from the very trust or savings you built for their future. That's not selfishness. That's reality.

That's why we say: You must include your own retirement planning as part of your child's special needs plan. The first step toward building your own retirement is knowing your own numbers. Let's start by calculating your own projected retirement expenses. How much will you need monthly? Will your mortgage be paid off? What will you spend on food, utilities, health insurance, and travel? Do you plan to support any other children or aging relatives? In this process, be sure to isolate what you need to spend on yourself and your spouse from what you spend on your child. While you may need to be prepared to spend both numbers, having an idea of whether Medicaid waivers or other sources can provide income or services for the benefit of your child is an important part of the planning process.

> **NOTE:** You can't care for someone else unless you've first secured your own oxygen mask.

Once you understand your baseline needs, you can layer on what's required to maintain your caregiving role. Will you continue to live with your child? Will you need a home aide as *you* age? Who will step in when your caregiving capacity diminishes? You must include care for you too.

We were recently reminded of the importance of this when a client went in for a minor surgery. She was going to have a week-long recovery, and she went through an extensive planning process to bring in other caregivers. The one detail she forgot was the middle of the night repositioning of her son with cerebral palsy. She found herself—against doctor's orders—moving her adult son in his bed to reposition him and keep him safe because she had forgotten to have someone else do it. This example is a great way to show all the unpaid supports we as parents provide—and how someone who cares for us may need to help care for our child as well.

Now let's align your savings with your goals. Many families assume they'll just "retire when it feels right." Or they look to achieve a certain number, without a real understanding of what that number means or how they need to budget within it. But special needs families don't have that luxury. You need to map out what your assets can support—and where the shortfalls may be.

As we figure out budget, you also need to think about what your budget is today. Look at how far away from retirement you are, and what your current savings levels are. Do you need to be saving more? Is there room in your budget to increase your savings rate?

Retirement Accounts

Understand the benefits of pre-tax versus post-tax qualified retirement accounts, and how those play a role in preparing your family for the future. A qualified retirement account is one that is covered by ERISA laws (Employee Retirement Income Security Act) and provides ways for people to save in a tax-advantaged way. The first step is to understand how these accounts may fit into your current budget.

Traditional retirement savings accounts, 401(k), 403b, SEP IRA, Simple IRA, and traditional IRA, all hold one thing in common: they use pre-tax money for the contributions, grow tax deferred (until distribution), and if held until age 59 ½, can be used without penalty. Tax will be paid when the money is withdrawn.

Retirement savings accounts with a Roth option are similar to the aforementioned accounts, with one key difference: they take post-tax money (money where appropriate taxes have already been paid) and go into a retirement savings account. Growth is deferred, and as long as the money is "seasoned" (meaning it's been in the account) for at least five years and the account owner is over age 59 ½, they can be withdrawn without penalty and without paying additional tax.

Both traditional and Roth retirement accounts are individual accounts that must be started by an individual. They require earned income to be deposited and used. Often, they will come with an employee match.

A rule of thumb: we always suggest that you maximize your employer matching funds. You can be tax efficient, have the best investment strategy available, and an incredibly solid savings plan—you still want to take advantage of every dollar that your employer will send your way in matching funds. So, if your employer offers a 3% match on your 401(k), make sure to take the 3% before taking advantage of Roth 401(k) options or other types of savings accounts.

When it comes to special needs planning, we *love* Roth IRAs more than any other type of investment when going toward a special needs trust. We know that most special needs planners are going to push you to leave traditional IRA and 401(k) funds to your trust to take advantage of the Stretch IRA (more to come on that). We see things differently.

The taxation of a trust makes it so that taking required minimum distributions—even stretched over a lifetime—very tricky. Trust tax rates very quickly reach the maximum tax bracket. A Roth IRA has no minimum distribution requirements at the time of writing this book—even inside a trust. The money can grow tax free and be distributed tax free—regardless of the trust tax rates or the individual's personal tax rate.

This being said, we don't know the specifics of your life and your tax situation. You should *always* consult a CPA and a special needs planner when working out how to be the most tax efficient with your savings and your trust planning.

Pensions and Survivor Benefits: Leveraging Traditional Retirement Income

For families lucky enough to have access to a pension, it can be a powerful tool in two-generation planning—especially when structured with a survivor benefit. These benefits are designed to continue providing income to a designated beneficiary after the pension holder's death, offering stability and predictability for dependents with disabilities.

If you're covered under a pension plan, the first step is to determine whether it includes a survivor benefit option. Many pensions—especially those from government, military, or legacy employers—offer the opportunity to continue payments to a spouse or dependent after your passing.

> **NOTE:** Ask your HR department about survivor benefits early—ideally well before retirement.

In families where a child with special needs is the dependent, survivor benefits can often be paid into a first-party special needs trust. This ensures that the income doesn't disrupt eligibility for government benefits like SSI or Medicaid. The trust must meet specific requirements (including Medicaid payback provisions and lack of contingent beneficiaries), but it's an option worth exploring.

For military families, there's additional flexibility. Under current CMS (Centers for Medicare & Medicaid Services) regulations, military Survivor Benefit Plan (SBP) payments can be directed to a first-party special needs trust, preserving government benefits while ensuring continuity of income. This requires following instructions published by the Defense Finance and Accounting Service (DFAS).[2]

If naming your child directly is not possible, you'll need to consider which option to select. Generally, your options are to elect a spousal survivor benefit (usually a reduced monthly benefit now in exchange for income for your spouse after your death) or taking the higher single-life annuity benefit and purchasing a life insurance policy to create a financial safety net.

It is really important that you work with your Human Resources department to understand fully what benefit options are available in the plan that you have. We also highly recommend that you consult with a special needs financial planner who can help you navigate the decision, keeping your child's best interests in mind while also understanding your own retirement needs.

Each decision has trade-offs, and there's no one-size-fits-all answer. These choices should be evaluated in light of your family's needs, health, financial goals, and overall planning strategy.

> **NOTE:** The right pension choice can provide decades of security for your loved one—choose wisely, and plan proactively.

Understanding Your Social Security Benefits

For parents planning over two generations, your own Social Security retirement benefits are a critical piece of the puzzle. Not only are they part of your future income stream—they may also unlock benefits for your child.

If your child qualifies as a **Disabled Adult Child (DAC)**—a designation we'll explore further in Chapter 6—they may be eligible to receive a benefit equal to up to 50% of your full retirement benefit while you are still alive, and up to 75% as a survivor benefit. This means the timing of when you claim your Social Security doesn't just impact your own retirement income, but potentially your child's financial support too.

We'll go deeper into the mechanics of DAC benefits soon, but for now, know this: delaying Social Security to increase your monthly benefit can also increase what your child receives. It's a powerful opportunity to provide support even after you're no longer earning.

That being said, delaying past full retirement age will not benefit your child—just one of the myriad ways that special needs planning is different than traditional planning where couples are often counseled to wait until age 70 to file for their benefits.

There are a few key factors for you to keep in mind here. First, make sure that you have gone to ssa.gov and pulled your Social Security earnings record and estimated benefit. This will estimate what your own benefit will be depending on at what age you take the benefit and give you some data you will need for determining what age you should retire at, when you file for Social Security, and what your child's benefit might be.

As with most government programs and agencies, there are a lot of acronyms and lingo used with Social Security benefits. Knowing the most important ones will be important. Primary Insurance Amount (PIA) is the amount you are eligible for at your Full Retirement Age (FRA) based on your earnings record. It's also important to know that Social Security retirement benefits, as well as Social Security Disability Income, are based on your earnings record and are not means-tested. This means your benefit will not be impacted by how much money you make or how much you have in assets. The same cannot be true for how they are taxed, but that is a whole different story.

This is also a good time to look at you and your spouse's Social Security benefits. If you both work, look at what each person's benefits are, your age differences, and what your family's total Social Security benefits may be. Working with a Social Security benefits advisor—or a team like All Needs Planning—is worth it when there are significant benefits involved.

For example, Social Security uses a complex formula to determine the family maximum benefit. This family maximum benefit includes what is paid to the wage earner, spouse of the wage earner, and any dependent beneficiaries. Knowing how this benefit will impact your spouse, and your child—especially if there are multiple dependent children—could mean a difference of thousands—and even millions, across the lifespan—in income to your family and your disabled child. Understanding the impact on your family isn't just important—it's a crucial part of your financial planning.

> **NOTE:** Your Social Security isn't just about your retirement—it could be your child's lifeline.

Health Savings Accounts (HSAs)

Now let us talk about a tool that is increasingly offered within employee benefit/medical insurance plans: the Health Savings Account. Do not confuse a Health Savings Account with a Flexible Spending Account, as they are different. While both provide an avenue for pre-tax savings, a Flexible Spending Account or FSA must be contributed to and spent within the calendar year (with some minor exceptions) or the money is lost. A Health Savings Account (HSA) is tied to a High-deductible Health Plan (HDHP) and is becoming more common as employers want their employees to bear more of the risk of their own health costs.

An HSA allows someone to put pre-tax funds into the account. Note that you must have the option of an HDHP in order to have access to an HSA, and the only way to have either of these is as an employee benefit—you cannot simply call a bank or an investment company and ask to open an HSA. The account is offered as a way for an employee to have access to a way to save in a tax-advantaged way for current or future healthcare costs.

Funds inside the account grow without paying tax as long as the funds are kept in the account. Many HSAs offer the ability to invest the funds after a certain amount has accumulated, with investment options varying by plan and offering.

This is another option that it is important you read through the offering document and work with your Human Resources department to understand exactly what benefits you have available to you. We can tell you generally how HSAs work, but you need to know the specifics and if this is an option available to you.

For families with high, ongoing healthcare costs, many choose to use funds from the HSA to cover their current needs. As you look at your budget, we encourage you to consider another option: paying for your costs from other sources and allowing your HSA savings to grow.

The reason? Funds inside an HSA are contributed with pre-tax funds (meaning you do not pay income tax on funds contributed), then they grow without paying tax on the growth, and *as long as they are used to pay healthcare expenses*, you do not pay taxes at the point of spend either.

You are also not required to spend the funds inside a calendar year. You can use them at any point in your life. For example, let's say you put $2,000 into your HSA today. Instead of paying for medical expenses with your HSA, you pay using other means and let the $2,000 grow. In 20 years, that $2,000 has grown to $8,000—and now you use it to cover part of your long-term care insurance premiums. (Yes, you can use HSA funds to cover long-term care insurance premiums, with limits and exceptions according to IRS guidelines.)

There is one extremely important aspect of HSA funds that you need to understand as they pertain to your family: you can use HSA funds for any member of your family's medical expenses *while you are alive*. However, current tax law makes it prohibitive for someone to inherit HSA funds. So even with the tax benefits, those are only helpful for one generation. So please, use your HSA if you can—and use it for your own retirement healthcare expenses—but know that it is not the best instrument to cover the future cost of care of your loved one with a disability.

ABLE Accounts: Autonomy and Flexibility

The ABLE account—short for the Stephen A. Beck Achieving a Better Life Experience Act of 2014—was created to allow individuals with disabilities to save money without affecting their eligibility for government benefits. The bill is named after a father who brainstormed a way to lift his disabled son out of poverty—and then advocated with lawmakers to get the bill passed. It is a program that has bipartisan support and continues to gain popularity as more families trust that the program is here to stay.

If the individual's disability began before age 26, they can open and manage an ABLE account. The account is established in their name and tied to their Social Security number—but acts as a shield, keeping them benefits eligible even if their assets go above $2,000 in the account—as long as the balance does not go above $100,000. Every dollar above $100,000 impacts eligibility for SSI.

> **NOTE:** The age of onset of disability will increase to age 46 on January 1, 2026, primarily to make the program open to veterans who were disabled by serving our country. That being said, you are not required to have served to be eligible for the ABLE account; anyone with any qualified disability can qualify for ABLE. Qualification is based on one of two factors: the individual is currently receiving SSI, *or* they have proof from a doctor of diagnosis of a disability that is expected to last their lifetime.

ABLE accounts are administered through each state's 529 program and come with powerful benefits. The earnings grow tax free—and when distributions/withdrawals are used for qualified disability expenses, they will be tax-free as well. Qualified disability expenses include housing, education, transportation, assistive technology, therapy, recreation, food, and much, much more. Daily spending and discretionary purchases can be used for an ABLE account. It can take gifts from family members or small inheritances (currently under $19,000).

The ABLE contribution used to be limited to the annual gift limit (plus more if the ABLE account holder was working and did not have access to a 401(k) or employer savings plan), but that guideline is changing in 2026. Be sure to look for the updated guidance from the IRS on exactly what the annual contribution limit will be.

One of our favorite benefits of the ABLE account is how it can be used to foster independence. An individual can manage their own spending with their ABLE account through debit cards, mobile apps, checkbooks, and online access (be sure to check the program specifics of the state program you are looking into, and know the applicable guidelines based on whether your loved one is under guardianship or not).

There are some benefits of ABLE that are available nationwide—and some that vary state to state. Some states offer tax benefits/deductions for putting money into an ABLE account. Abletoday.org is a great resource for figuring out what your state's benefits will be—and if your state program is the right one for you.

> **NOTE:** ABLE accounts are about more than savings. They're about dignity, autonomy, and quality of life.

One powerful strategy we recommend is to include language in a special needs trust that allows funds to be transferred to an ABLE account each year. That way, the individual can access a set amount for flexible use—without jeopardizing government benefits.

We also often work with families who began saving for their loved one's future education using a 529 college savings plan, only to later realize that a traditional college experience may not be realistic. For these families, there's good news: they can roll over unused 529 funds into an ABLE account, up to the annual contribution limit (again, be sure to check current IRS guidelines for what the annual contribution is). This provides much more flexibility—ABLE accounts can be used for a wide range of qualified disability expenses, not just education.

OPTIMIZING TOOLS FOR FINANCIAL PLANNING: WHAT GOES WHERE

Each of these accounts and income streams behaves differently depending on your age, income, and withdrawal needs. The right strategy is highly personalized—but the common thread is *intentionality*. You must decide which accounts are for *you*, and which are for *your child*, and balance your contributions accordingly.

As you determine your financial plan for both yourself and your child, you want to keep these major factors in mind: your retirement income needs, your child's cost-of-care needs over their lifetime, other large known expenses such as car purchases, and goals such as vacations, purchase of a second home, paying for weddings/college/etc. for other siblings, and more.

Then go back to these budgetary concerns and write down every asset and account that you currently have, what it's expected growth is, how it is currently invested (if appropriate), and how it is taxed right now versus how it will be taxed to your child inside their special needs trust. You may need to consult with a special needs financial planner and certified public accountant to obtain this information. Then look at all of your different income streams and when you plan to take them. How much income do you have for your own retirement? Is there enough to cover both your own and your child's?

If there is not enough, take a look back at your retirement income needs and goals. Are there areas that need to shift? For example, if you were looking to purchase a second home, could you change that to be a budget for vacation instead? In essence, you are playing a game of not only putting together a puzzle but also pulling different levers until the puzzle pieces fit together. Figuring out what needs to change and shift to meet your goals is crucial.

Take a look also at the timing of when different income streams come into play. From Social Security, to pension income, to taking required minimum distributions, have the knowledge and then develop strategy around what might work best. For example, you may retire from your job at age 65—in order to retain your employer's medical insurance until Medicare kicks in at age 65. However, you may opt to not start receiving your pension and Social Security until age 67. For those two years, you live off savings that you have in taxable accounts, not touching your retirement accounts. During this window, it may make sense to look at doing IRA to Roth IRA conversions. Your family may be in a lower tax bracket, where you can convert and take advantage of paying the lower tax rate, and optimize your retirement accounts for future inheritance into your child's special needs trust.

Table 5.1 describes the tools we most often use in multigenerational financial plans. We have gone through what the different tools are. This table summarizes the different tools and how each would fit into a holistic, multigenerational special needs financial plan. You will notice one tool that we have not discussed so far: life insurance. In the next chapter

Table 5.1 Toolbox for Special Needs Financial Planning

Financial Tool	Purpose	Tax Treatment	Best Use Case
ABLE Account	Savings in the individual's name	Tax-free growth if used for disability expenses	Small-scale, daily expenses and autonomy.
Special Needs Trust	Hold inheritance/assets without losing benefits	Varies but generally highest tax rate	Long-term savings; structured distributions; can own home(s), vehicle(s) and more.
Pre-tax Retirement Savings	Wage earners can deposit retirement savings and often have employer matched funds available	Pre-tax money; growth is not taxed—ordinary income tax is paid when distributions are made past age 59.5	Parents retirement savings; can be used to fund a special needs trust and care should be used to keep Secure Act restrictions in mind.
Roth Retirement Savings	Post-tax retirement savings	Tax-free growth and withdrawal	Parents' retirement with child's future in mind.

(Continued)

Table 5.1 (Continued)

Financial Tool	Purpose	Tax Treatment	Best Use Case
Pensions	Retirement income paid by government or company to a worker who reaches certain eligibility requirements	Taxed when paid to the beneficiary	Generally provides income replacement in retirement for a wage earner; sometimes survivor benefits can be named.
Life Insurance	Lump-sum payout to fund trust or estate	Generally tax-free to beneficiaries	Replaces income; supplements inheritance.

we are going to discuss in-depth the process of budgeting and forecasting what you need in your own retirement and what your child will need during their lifetime. We will then look at the different assets and income streams you will have available to you across both lifetimes. Once this process is done, we will walk you through how to figure out what gaps are in place. This is important because one of the most important tools available for filling gaps is life insurance. Understanding both the tools that are available with life insurance, when to implement, and how to fit them into your overall budget is incredibly important—and covered in depth in Chapter 8.

> **NOTE:** The right combination of tools can turn a patchwork plan into a powerful legacy.

Special Needs Trusts

Special needs trusts are a tool that—while not exactly a financial planning tool—are still important to know and understand. Their purpose in special needs planning is to hold assets in trust for the person with a disability, while keeping them benefits eligible and providing a trustee who is an appointed fiduciary. Understanding how they work, the fiduciary relationship of the trustee, and more—from the legal side—are discussed in detail in Chapter 9. For the purposes of this chapter, we want to discuss the financial planning aspects of a special needs trust.

The most important thing to know about a special needs trust is to decide when to fund it, what to fund it with, and how to invest once the funds are there. In most cases, we recommend that you fund the trust at your death. However, this is a highly personal decision—and one that you should consult with your financial planner and attorney to discuss specific options. You may wish to fund a special needs trust prior to your death. For example, if you are purchasing a home for your child to live in, you may wish to put the home into the special needs trust at the time of purchase. However, you should understand that a trust is a separate entity, and you need to review how your trust is taxed (another discussion with your attorney), whether you need to file a tax return, and what other reporting requirements there may be.

Next you need to think about what to fund the trust with. Being aware of how retirement assets work inside a trust is incredibly important. With the right trust language, the Secure Act (discussed in detail in Chapter 9), allows an inherited qualified retirement account (with pre-tax money) to stretch minimum distributions over the disabled beneficiary's lifetime. It is crucial that you are working with an elder law attorney who is experienced in writing special needs trusts and also familiar with current estate planning tax laws—the Secure Act is the most recent at the time of publication of the book but know that any new legislation might address this and should be looked into.

Under the Secure Act, a Roth IRA has the most ideal tax treatment. The money is post-tax from the wage earner, grows without paying tax on the growth, and then (as long as seasoned appropriately more than five years) can be taken out without paying additional tax. There is no required minimum distribution for the original wage earner or for a disabled beneficiary, including inside of the special needs trust. We highly recommend prioritizing Roth IRA assets as inheritance inside special needs trusts.

Life insurance can be another tax-efficient way to fund a special needs trust. The funds come in tax free and can be invested in whatever way the trustee decides. The policies are generally payable right away, which could be crucial for a beneficiary who needs an inflow of cash to keep them safe and supported while the overall estate is settled. This can be especially important as some estates can take a year or more to settle. Life insurance is also the best way to fund any gaps that you have uncovered in making sure your loved one's cost of care is paid for throughout their lifetime.

And last (but certainly not least), it is incredibly important that you reach out to family and have the uncomfortable conversation of whether or not they plan to support your loved one in their estate plan. Sometimes this is easier—grandparents may already be involved in the daily supports and financial needs your family has. They may be more open to a conversation. Others may not want to discuss it. Having a plan for the discussion—and declaring openly that you have zero expectations but do need to put together a plan—can help you know exactly how to prepare, including helping provide them legal instructions during the estate planning process for how to name the special needs trust as a beneficiary.

Multigenerational financial planning may also include aunts, uncles, great grandparents, cousins, and more—depending on your situation. We strongly recommend having a family meeting—or a series of family meetings, depending on personalities, circumstances, and how people might react in discussing finances—where you can have an open agenda to discuss your child's needs, discuss the importance of them not inheriting money directly, and asking for not a direct request for help—unless you are comfortable with that and feel it is important—but a clear direction on how your child may be named and if an inheritance may be coming to them. This information will help you stay armed and will also help you know who may be open to having a more supportive role in your child's life and future.

> **NOTE:** If this is feeling overwhelming, don't worry. We're in this together, one step at a time.

FINANCIAL PLANNING MILESTONES FOR SPECIAL NEEDS FAMILIES

We have talked mostly about the steps you need to take to prepare for your retirement and the lifetime of your loved one. Table 5.2 breaks down steps you can take in stages, depending on the age of your loved one and how close you are to retirement. There are many variables here to acknowledge: the diagnosis and care needs of your loved one, how old you are, how close you are to retirement, and so much more. The aim of this book is to provide you with education—so that when you do seek advice, you are paying specifically for advice and not for education.

> **NOTE:** Good planning isn't a one-time act. It's a series of thoughtful steps, taken in the right order.

WHEN THE CAREGIVER NEEDS CARE: MEDICAL AND LONG-TERM PLANNING FOR PARENTS

One of the hardest truths we face in special needs planning is this: the caregiver will eventually need care. Whether it's you or your spouse, most of us will reach a point in life when we need help with daily tasks, health management, or mobility. And just like we plan for our child's long-term care needs, we must plan for our own.

Hard truth: if your child is living with you at the point where you start needing care, this could create a crisis—not only for providing you and them care, but also in the disruption to their daily routines that they now have to go through without your help and guidance.

Table 5.2 Timeline for Financial Planning

Life Stage/Planning Phase	Parent Actions	Child/Dependent Actions
Early Years of Diagnosis or Planning	• Build emergency fund • Explore ABLE account • Consider life insurance • Open Roth IRA if eligible	• Document care needs • Track diagnosis for benefit eligibility
School-age Years/Growing Complexity	• Increase retirement contributions • Begin trust and estate planning • Discuss future caregiving roles with family	• Use IEP and transition planning • Join waitlists for Medicaid waiver programs
Transition to Adulthood	• Finalize special needs trust • Revisit financial and legal plans • Assess cost of care and housing options	• Apply for SSI/SSDI • Develop independent living skills

(Continued)

Table 5.2 *(Continued)*

Life Stage/ Planning Phase	Parent Actions	Child/Dependent Actions
Preretirement Planning	• Consider Roth conversions or life insurance • Reassess retirement income strategy	• Solidify supported employment/ housing • Use ABLE account for expenses
Retirement and Beyond	• Claim Social Security • Implement succession plan for care • Coordinate trust distributions	• Maintain eligibility for DAC/ Medicaid • Continue community engagement and care supports

This reality adds complexity to financial planning. You're not only saving to support your child throughout their lifetime—you also need to prepare for the possibility that your own healthcare or living costs may rise dramatically as you age. That's why long-term care planning is an essential part of any two-generation financial strategy.

While we will dive more into long-term care insurance in Chapter 8, we want you to know that it's one potential tool for paying for long-term care—one of the best in terms of leveraging your existing funding while not eating into the funds needed for your child.

Some families use dedicated savings, others rely on insurance, and some make arrangements with adult children or trusted professionals. What matters most is that you plan for it.

> **NOTE:** Most caregivers don't plan to need care—but according to the former Administration for Community Living, just under 70% of families need and use long-term care.[3] Your child's future depends on your ability to plan for your own.

While we are on this topic, I also want to encourage you to think through the timing of your own retirement and how you will access general healthcare. Make sure that if there is a gap between when you retire and when you can access Medicare, that you have a plan and savings to address the gap. Once you use Medicare, make sure you have a plan for the costs that Medicare does not cover. We do not suggest using Medicare Advantage policies because they severely limit the number of providers available to you, often do not approve needed care, and may kick you off the plan later if you get sick—or require medical underwriting to stay on the plan. Consulting with a licensed Medicare insurance provider is highly recommended.

Ignoring your own future needs could have a ripple effect: if you end up needing care and haven't planned for it, you may inadvertently use the same resources your child is counting on. We've seen estates drained by unexpected health crises, leaving dependent children without sufficient funds. It's heartbreaking—and preventable.

So, what does planning for your own long-term care involve? Make sure you think ahead about where you want to live and who will care for you. Get an assessment of your home to see if it can be adapted for you and your spouse to age in place. Identify potential costs and funding sources—and talk to a planner about how those costs might be covered—through insurance, assets, or a combination. And make sure those plans are documented alongside your child.

This is a great time to start thinking about your living will and medical directive as well—you'll learn more about that in Chapter 10—so start thinking about what your wishes for your own care and how you want to be treated in case of an ongoing medical emergency or healthcare need, where you may not be able to verbally tell others what you want/need.

This is the heart of two-generation financial planning: ensuring the caregiver is cared for so that the child with disabilities is never left unsupported.

> **NOTE:** Your well-being is not separate from your child's plan—it's a cornerstone of it.

BRINGING IT ALL TOGETHER: A TWO-GENERATION APPROACH TO FINANCIAL PLANNING

When we talk about financial planning over two generations, we aren't just talking about numbers on a spreadsheet. We're talking about legacies, relationships, and the everyday realities of caregiving—all woven into a plan that honors the needs of your loved one *and* your own life's journey.

The truth is that most families don't plan because they're overwhelmed. The system is confusing. The terminology is dense. The stakes are high.

But planning doesn't have to be perfect to be powerful.

> **NOTE:** A plan you build today—even if it's not perfect—is better than a crisis tomorrow.

A robust two-generation plan is grounded in a realistic cost-of-care analysis. It's supported by government benefits and smart tax strategies. It's designed to preserve your child's long-term quality of life, includes your own retirement and healthcare needs, and fully takes advantage of appropriate tools such as ABLE accounts, Roth IRAs, Social Security, and life insurance.

More importantly, it's built with love, wisdom, and support. Let's be clear: you don't have to do this alone. There are professionals who understand your situation, families who have walked this path, and tools that are more accessible than ever.

> **NOTE:** For a financial planning checklist, visit www.allneedsplanning.com/templates/financialchecklist and use code **TWO-GEN-READY**.

We'll continue to build out the financial strategies in later chapters, but as we leave this one, remember this: special needs financial planning is not just about money. It's about building a life with dignity—for your loved one and for yourself.

FINAL THOUGHTS

When we first started helping families with special needs financial planning, we thought it was about numbers: How much to save. How to invest. What tools to use. And all of that is important. But as we've walked alongside hundreds of families—and built our own plans for people we love—we've learned that financial planning is also deeply emotional.

We're not just talking about asset allocation. We're talking about legacy. We're talking about the sacred responsibility of loving someone who depends on you—maybe not just today but for the rest of their life.

This chapter might have felt heavy. That's okay. It's a heavy topic. But here's what we want you to take away: you're not alone. This kind of planning isn't easy, but it is possible. And when you take the time to build a plan that looks two generations ahead, you are doing something deeply courageous and loving.

You are saying: "I see you. I plan for you. And I believe in a future where you are supported and safe—even when I'm no longer here."

That's not just financial planning. That's love in action.

Chapter 6

Government Benefits and Special Needs Planning

When you're building a long-term plan for a loved one with a disability, you can't do it alone—and you're not supposed to. Government benefit programs exist to provide essential support for individuals and families who need help covering healthcare, income, housing, and services across a lifetime. These programs make it possible to afford care, access support, and create a more stable future for your loved one and your family.

For many families, government benefits are not just part of the plan—they're the foundation. Medicaid may cover a personal care aide. Supplemental Security Income (SSI) might help pay rent or groceries. A Medicaid waiver could open the door to job coaching, behavioral therapy, or supported living. Without these supports, a financial plan often won't stretch far enough. And even more than that, even with unlimited funds, many of these supports are not available outside of these government benefit pathways.

In this chapter, we'll walk you through the most essential government benefits for families supporting someone with a disability. From Medicaid/Medicaid Waivers and Medicare to Social Security and SSI, you'll get a crash course in government benefits and programs and how they might apply to your family.

We'll also show you how these programs interact, what steps to take to apply, and how to advocate through the red tape. Our goal is to make this complex landscape more understandable—and more manageable.

> **NOTE:** Don't overlook government benefits—they're not just backup plans; they're vital tools for long-term support.

THE SAFETY NET: WHY GOVERNMENT BENEFITS MATTER

Government benefit programs weren't created overnight—they were built in response to real human needs, especially poverty and the many challenges that come with it, like illness, unemployment, and unstable housing. These programs have evolved over the decades, shaped by changing times and priorities.

Let's rewind to the 1930s. In the middle of the Great Depression, President Franklin D. Roosevelt signed the Social Security Act of 1935—then called the Economic Security Act—to help older adults and those who could no longer work. Taxes to support this system began in 1937, and regular monthly payments soon followed. Initially, Social Security only provided retirement benefits, but by 1939, it expanded to include survivors and dependents. Fast forward to 1956, and disability benefits entered the picture.

In 1965, President Lyndon B. Johnson declared a "War on Poverty," and two major programs were born: Medicare (health coverage for people 65 and older) and Medicaid (health coverage for low-income individuals). Medicaid was introduced through Title XIX of the Social Security Act and allowed states to provide essential health coverage to people who otherwise couldn't afford it.

Even though these programs were created at the federal level, they are managed by individual states. That means the rules and qualifications can vary depending on where you live—which can make understanding and accessing benefits confusing at times.

Behind the scenes, the Centers for Medicare & Medicaid Services (CMS) is the federal agency that sets guidelines, regulations, and funding structures for Medicaid. While CMS provides oversight and partial funding, each state decides how to implement those programs. States—and in some cases, local governments—design their own waiver programs, define eligibility criteria, and determine the specific services offered. That's why a service available in one state may not exist in another or may require a completely different application process.

> **NOTE:** While the intent behind government benefits is clear—to support people in need—the reality is sometimes messy.

Many families find the application process confusing and frustrating. Websites can be hard to navigate. Knowing what to ask for (and how to ask) is not always obvious. And sadly, reports of fraud and misuse mean that legitimate applicants often face extra scrutiny. It's a system full of good intentions but also filled with complexity. Your experience may vary widely based on timing, location, and your individual needs.

We work with families where Medicaid waivers have allowed both parents to work full time, run a small business, attend their other children's events, and even plan family vacations—things that once felt completely out of reach. The supports provided through waiver services—such as in-home care, respite, and community integration programs—can transform daily life from survival mode to something more sustainable and joyful. With the right waiver in place, families often tell us they finally feel like they can breathe again, reclaiming parts of their identity and relationships that had been on hold for years.

UNDERSTANDING THE MEDICAID WAIVER

Medicaid's Home and Community-based Services (HCBS) waivers were designed to help individuals with disabilities receive services in their homes and communities rather than institutions. The guidelines were provided by the Center for Medicaid and Medicare Services, offering a framework for states to build offerings outside of traditional Medicaid that supported individuals with institutions.

The reasoning was threefold: one, to avoid the very real human catastrophe of institutions like Willowbrook; two, the numbers make sense: the Department of Financing estimates care can be provided within a community setting at the same or lower rate for individuals with disabilities than in an institutional setting; and three, allowing an individual to preserve their relationships with family and community is preferable to forcing them to live separate and isolated. Families prefer to have their loved ones at home and, with some support, are willing to share the economic and support needs with others.

Having that support also allows many families to work, start businesses, support other children, and be more involved in their community because they have more space, time, and money to give back.

The waiver part comes into play through Section 1915(c) of the Social Security Act, which allows states to apply for waivers to provide services not typically covered under the Medicaid program, particularly those provided in home and community settings.[1] At the time of publication, they are governed by CMS (Center for Medicare and Medicaid Services). Previously they received heavy guidance from the Administration for Community Living, which has been disbanded.

Services offered by Home and Community-based Services waivers include respite care (meaning giving parents some relief and rest), in-home support staff, day programs, job coaching and supported employment, community integration programs, transportation assistance, and much, much more.

According to the Kaiser Family Foundation, 75% of Medicaid HCBS enrollees live with family caregivers.

This isn't just a quality-of-life issue—it's economic. Without these supports, many individuals are at risk of institutionalization, and families face staggering care costs. We have spoken to countless families who were unable to have a two-earner household because of the costs of caring for their child.

Getting a Waiver: Where Advocacy Begins

Every state administers its own waiver system. You may see a state offer multiple waivers for different diagnoses, care needs, or age groups. There could be years (or even decades) long waitlists. And eligibility requirements and application processes can vary widely.

The following are the general steps to obtaining a waiver.

First, contact your state's Medicaid Waiver Office. It may have different names in different states, which makes it even more confusing. In Virginia, the waivers themselves are called the Developmental Disability waiver or, if you need nursing and living supports only, the CCC+ or long-term care waiver. Each of these waiver systems has different contacts. In Washington state, it's the DDA waiver. If you're having trouble finding it, you could also search for "Home and Community-based Services in (your state)."

Once you have found the appropriate person, ask the question: *"Which waiver program is appropriate for my family member?"* And don't stop with simply asking. Contact a local advocacy organization—your developmental disability council, your state's version of PEATC (Parent Education and Advocacy Training Center), or us to figure out which waiver your family is best suited for. Often, you must go in knowing what you want instead of asking for a menu or guidance. Unfortunately, this information is not widely published or disseminated, making it even more difficult for families to navigate.

Now you must complete an intake and eligibility assessment. Sometimes, you will go into an office and provide paperwork. Other times, someone will come to your home and do an assessment. It varies from state to state, region to region, city to city even.

Many states tie Medicaid waiver eligibility to SSI eligibility—meaning, you must be eligible for SSI first, in order to be eligible for a Medicaid waiver. Sometimes, the financial qualifications for a Medicaid waiver are even more restrictive than those for SSI. Know the rules in your state before you apply—if your child has more than $2,000 in their bank account at the time of application, they would be immediately disqualified, and their application may not be looked at further.

When you are doing this, make sure to ask about waitlist processes. Sometimes you have to redo the paperwork every year. Other times you go into a portal and fill out a form stating that you are still interested.

Importantly, keep all documentation organized. We suggest starting an advocacy book. Have a section just for the Medicaid paperwork. And put an envelope or a catch-all space by your doorstep to put all incoming mail in—we promise, there will be a lot.

Most of all—don't assume you're ineligible. Many families are told they make too much money—but the waiver programs are for *the person with the disability*, not based on parent income—even before the age of 18. That's one reason it's called a waiver program—it waives the income and asset requirements for the household because the person has a lifelong disability.

If your child is put on a waitlist, this is where advocacy comes in. Make sure you respond to requests for information when they come. Know what your rights—and responsibilities—are. If you have access to a case manager, text them frequently—at least once a month—especially providing any medical or health updates. If there is a job loss, a difficulty with education/school, a parent is sick with a long-term illness, these are all issues to let your case manager know about. Their job is to advocate for you—and they often have a caseload of hundreds—so it helps to be top of mind, and let them know in detail the challenges you are facing.

Getting on a waitlist does more than just provide the option for future support—it makes sure that there is a safety net in place if the unthinkable happens—where you are not available to care for your child unexpectedly. The state jumps in, and the child becomes a priority for a Medicaid waiver. This can be a very important safety net protecting vulnerable individuals.

Personal advocacy is important—pushing for change at a local, state, and federal level is important too. Share your experiences with your local city council, your state representatives, and your federal representatives. Hearing from you really does make a difference.

> **NOTE:** Waiver eligibility isn't always intuitive—ask your case manager about functional and financial qualifications.

Case Study: Jason's Waiver Path

Jason is a 19-year-old young man with autism. He has emerging independence but still needs help with daily hygiene, social behavior, and staying on task. His parents, Ann and Mitch, applied for a Medicaid waiver that supports young adults building life skills. Although Jason qualified, he was placed on a waitlist. While they waited, they also applied for SSI and collected documentation to strengthen his case. When Jason's name eventually came up, he was ready—with a team already in place to help him transition toward independent living. It's important to note that once you receive a waiver, you have to be ready to use it. Without regular use, you could lose the waiver and go right back on the waitlist—or never be offered it again. Make sure this does not happen to you!

Keep in mind also that Medicaid waiver programs are *optional* for states to provide. Not all states have waiver programs. The Center for Medicare and Medicaid Services provides guidelines for these programs but does not require states to offer them. As federal funding ebbs and flows, staying on top of what your state is committed to offering—and what they have the budget for—is crucial.

> **NOTE:** Don't wait until crisis hits—get on the waiver list early and gather your documentation now.

TRADITIONAL MEDICAID: A CRITICAL SUPPORT SYSTEM—EVEN WITHOUT A WAIVER

Traditional Medicaid is the backbone of healthcare coverage for many individuals with disabilities. Even if your loved one isn't eligible for a Medicaid waiver—or is stuck on a waitlist—traditional Medicaid can still offer essential medical and therapeutic support.

Traditional Medicaid covers—you guessed it—medical needs. It can act as primary or secondary insurance for millions of Americans who are eligible either through financial means or through disability.

Medicaid expansion—through the Affordable Care Act—expanded access to Medicaid and healthcare for millions of Americans with disabilities who did not qualify for a Medicaid waiver. We sometimes call these people "in-betweeners" (this is not an official term).

Medicaid may cover primary care and specialist visits, hospital stays and emergency care, prescription medications, mental health services, durable medical equipment (like wheelchairs or walkers), and some therapies like speech, occupational, and physical therapy. Many do not realize that when someone is eligible for a Medicaid waiver, they *also* have access to traditional Medicaid. And it may not be called Medicaid in your state—many states have their own name for it, and some have contracts with private companies. So, you may have a Blue Cross Blue Shield health policy, for example, that is actually giving you Medicaid coverage.

There are certain Medicaid income and asset limits that vary state by state, and with the recent passage of the One Big Beautiful Bill, Medicaid guidelines (and especially, Medicaid expansion guidelines) are being updated as we speak. Staying on top of these changes will be important to your family. One way to stay on top of them is to join our Learning Lab—where we will be keeping people up to date with all changes as they come to fruition.

While it doesn't offer the full scope of services that waivers provide—such as in-home caregiving, community-based employment, or behavioral supports—it's still a foundational benefit that helps cover many necessary healthcare needs.

Medicaid and Medicaid Waiver programs differ in their scope of services, care settings, eligibility requirements, and enrollment processes. Medicaid Waiver programs give states the flexibility to use federal matching funds to provide services.

In most states, qualifying for SSI will automatically qualify your loved one for traditional Medicaid. But even without SSI, individuals may still be eligible for Medicaid based on income, disability status, or participation in other programs (like foster care or adoption assistance).

Some families are surprised to learn that traditional Medicaid alone can be enough to support someone's medical needs—especially in early adulthood. It might not cover everything, but it can make an enormous difference.

Keep in mind that if your child isn't on a waiver yet, don't panic. Traditional Medicaid is still a powerful tool—use what's available now while you plan for what's next. Waiver or no waiver, don't overlook what traditional Medicaid can provide—it may be your bridge to long-term support.

Table 6.1 provides a summary comparison of Medicaid Waivers to Traditional Medicaid—and what each provide.

Table 6.1   Medicaid Waivers Versus Traditional Medicaid

Feature	Medicaid Waivers	Traditional Medicaid
Purpose	Provide community-based support to avoid institutionalization	Cover basic medical services and healthcare
Flexibility	Highly customizable; may include behavioral, vocational, and home supports	Standardized healthcare coverage (doctors, hospitals, medications)
Eligibility	Often based on diagnosis or level of need; sometimes waives income rules	Income and asset limits apply strictly
Waitlist	Yes, in most states	No waitlist
Services Covered	Personal care aides, job coaching, day programs, respite care	Hospital visits, primary care, emergency services
Administered by	State Medicaid agency or local agencies	State Medicaid agency

> **NOTE:** Waivers supplement Medicaid—they don't replace it. Most families will use both to build a complete support system.

UNDERSTANDING SOCIAL SECURITY BENEFITS

Social Security programs are like a safety net designed to catch people in times of need. But before that net can open, you have to go through an application process, prove eligibility, and then stay in compliance. It's a process that involves forms, interviews, document-gathering, and a lot of patience. The system is national, but it serves individuals—so, yes, it can feel impersonal, slow, and frustrating at times.

SSI is a monthly cash assistance program for individuals with very low income and limited resources. It's designed to supplement whatever income the person already has. In most states, qualifying for SSI also means automatic eligibility for Medicaid. SSI is a means-tested benefit—at the time of publication, you must make less than and have less than $2,000 in countable assets for an individual; $3,000 for a couple. According to ssa.gov, an adult must make less than $2,020/month from a job to be eligible for SSI or have less than $988 per month from nonwork sources, like unemployment or pensions.

Some states have higher limits due to cost-of-living adjustments. There are certain exceptions to the income limit as well. For example, SNAP benefits, Section 8 housing vouchers, rent rebates or property tax refunds, and Temporary Assistance for Needy Families (TANF) do not count toward the income limit. In addition, Impairment-related Work Expenses (IRWE) do not count for people with disabilities who are working. We will talk later in this chapter about the

Ticket to Work program, an important way to receive SSI and be supported by the program while working and making higher wages.

It is important to consult ssa.gov and the Program Operating Manual System (POMS) to see current rules for SSI—they are updated frequently. An important and helpful recent update was a technology overhaul that is allowing for faster and accessible in-person appointments at Social Security offices. Staying on top of changes can be a full-time job—but it's an important one. Stay in touch with your local advocacy offices, join our Learning Lab, or look at the POMS to stay on top of the rule changes.

What to Bring to an SSI Appointment

When preparing for an SSI appointment, it's important to gather documentation that clearly demonstrates your child's disability and financial need. Be sure to have as much documentation on hand as possible. We recommend the following:

- The most recent psychological evaluation or diagnosis
- Individualized Education Plans (IEPs)
- School transition assessments
- Medical records or provider letters confirming diagnosis and treatment
- A list of medications
- Proof of household income and resources
- Bank statements and any financial accounts in the child's name
- Lease agreements or rental arrangements (see following text)

It is important to use Social Security's Disability Starter Kit to guide your documentation process—it's available online at ssa.gov.

Receiving the Full SSI Amount Through a Business Arrangement

If your loved one is living at home and not paying full rent or household costs, their SSI payment may be reduced due to what Social Security calls "in-kind support and maintenance." However, if you establish a formal business arrangement—such as a lease agreement where the individual pays a set amount for room and board—this reduction can be avoided.

The standard formula is known as the One-third Reduction Rule. But if the individual pays one-third of the Presumed Maximum Value (PMV) plus $20 per month, they can qualify for the full Federal Benefit Rate (FBR). This arrangement must be clearly documented and consistent. At the time of publication, a lease agreement in the amount of $350 covers the PMV plus $20. Be sure to know what the exact number is when you go to apply by checking the Social Security Program Operating Manual System (POMS).

Keep in mind that a formal business arrangement—in other words, a lease—will require the receiving party (you, or the person who issued the lease) to declare that rental income on their taxes. Discuss this with your CPA, and make sure you know what the consequences will be. We usually find the taxable consequences to be negligible but cannot speak for your specific situation.

> **NOTE:** Treat your child's living arrangement like any other rental—clear terms, regular payments, and written agreements help preserve benefits. For a lease template, go to our website at www.allneedsplanning.com/templates/lease and enter the code: LEASE.

Social Security Disability Insurance (SSDI) is for adults who have worked and paid into Social Security and then become disabled. Disabled Adult Child (DAC) benefits are for individuals whose disability began before age 22 and are based on a parent's Social Security work record. It is important to note that neither SSDI nor the DAC benefit are means-tested benefits. However, it is important that in many states, even if you are receiving SSDI, you still must show that you would be eligible for SSI in order to receive a Medicaid waiver.

> **NOTE:** A disability determination before age 22 is critical—don't delay applying if your child qualifies. It is important to show that your child's disability started before age 18. And don't fall trap to the idea that a genetic disorder will automatically be accepted as having begun at birth—the right process still has to be followed.

Understanding DAC and SSDI

Table 6.2 summarizes SSI, SSDI, and the DAC benefit. While all run by the Social Security Administration, and all are federal programs, they are enacted in different ways. SSI is a means-tested benefit, while SSDI is based off the person's own work record. The SSDI-DAC benefit is an adult dependent claiming off a qualified adult's work record (usually the parent) once the parent files for their own Social Security benefit.

One really important component of the DAC benefit: the child's disability determination must show that their disability started before age 18 and is expected to continue throughout their lifetime and prohibit them from working. Additionally, the adult whose benefit will be providing for the child must state when they file for their own benefit that they have a disabled adult child. This is especially important for divorced parents to be aware of: they may not physically have custody of their adult child, but they can still greatly impact the child's benefits.

Table 6.2 SSI, SSDI, and the DAC Benefit

Program	Who Qualifies	Based On	Benefits	Other Notes
SSI	Individuals with disabilities and low income/resources	Financial need	Up to $967/month (2025 FBR)	Often comes with automatic Medicaid depending on the state
SSDI	Adults with work history who become disabled	Own work record	Varies based on work history	Medicare begins after two years of SSDI
DAC	Adults with a disability that began before age 22	Parent's work record	Up to 50% of parent's benefit (or up to 75% if parent is deceased)	Eligibility depends on parent's retirement, disability, or death

The following is the DAC eligibility checklist:

- Disability must have started before age 22.
- Cannot be married (unless to another person with a disability also receiving DAC).
- Cannot have substantial gainful activity (SGA) income.
- Must prove disability through SSA's evaluation process.
- Parent must be receiving retirement, disability, or survivor benefits.

How DAC Fits into Your Planning

DAC is often the single most valuable Social Security benefit available to a person with a lifelong disability. Because it is not means-tested like SSI, the income level is often higher, and it opens the door to Medicare after two years of eligibility.

A common misstep is missing the documentation window for proving the disability began before age 22. Once missed, it can be very hard to retroactively correct—so early application, often during the 18–22 age range, is key.

It is also important to understand the income limits for the Medicaid waiver and how your state's waiver program interacts with the DAC program. Switching from SSI to a DAC benefit alone is not enough to remove eligibility for the Medicaid waiver program; however, if there are other income sources involved, it could be. Some states have worked with the Center for Medicare and Medicaid to disregard the SSDI-DAC income even with other sources of income; others have not. Know your state's laws and also know this: while Social Security does not always automatically switch someone from SSI to SSDI-DAC, you cannot legally stop them from switching someone from SSI to SSDI-DAC on a parents' record. And there is pressure to move away from the means-tested benefit (SSI) to the non-means-tested benefit.

Knowing the systems, processes, and what is available is the first step to being able to care for your loved one. Being able to plug them into the right programs for them is the next step.

How DAC and SSI Interact

Many individuals with disabilities start out on SSI as young adults. Then, when a parent retires, becomes disabled, or passes away, the individual may become eligible for DAC

(Disabled Adult Child) benefits—based on the parent's Social Security work record. This benefit often exceeds the SSI amount and may trigger eligibility for Medicare.

If someone receives DAC benefits, they may no longer qualify for SSI, since SSI is based on financial need and DAC is not. However, some individuals receive both, especially if the DAC amount is lower than the SSI benefit. In those cases, SSI may "top off" the benefit up to the full amount.

Why is this important? Because SSI is often the gateway to Medicaid. When someone loses SSI due to receiving DAC, it's essential to make sure that the regional Social Security office still shows the beneficiary as eligible for SSI, even if not receiving—so that their Medicaid and Medicaid waiver status is not interrupted. Many states are grappling with this issue now and are working with CMS (Center for Medicaid and Medicare Services, the national umbrella that sets federal policies for Medicaid and Medicare) to find commonsense solutions.

Case Study: From SSI to DAC—Building a Bridge to Long-term Support

When Olivia turned 18, her parents, Monica and Jay, were ready. They had already assembled a binder of her school IEPs, psychological evaluations, therapy notes, and a letter from her pediatric neurologist confirming her intellectual disability diagnosis from early childhood. Olivia, who had always lived at home, was about to exit the school system's transition program and begin a day program supported by a Medicaid waiver.

Monica and Jay filed for SSI as soon as Olivia was legally considered an adult. Because she had no income or resources of her own, and because they set up a lease agreement where she paid one-third PMV + $20 for her room and board, she was approved for the full monthly SSI amount.

At first, Olivia received Medicaid automatically through SSI approval. But Monica and Jay weren't just thinking short term—they had an eye on what would happen when they retired. Olivia's disability had started well before age 22, so she would eventually qualify for DAC benefits when either Monica or Jay began collecting Social Security themselves.

Fast forward seven years. Monica retired at age 62, and Olivia's SSI shifted to DAC status. Because Monica's retirement benefit was $2,200/month, Olivia began receiving 50% of that—$1,100/month—under DAC, replacing her SSI. Importantly, this meant Olivia now qualified for Medicare, in addition to Medicaid.

The extra monthly income helped cover additional therapies and hobbies Olivia enjoyed. The family felt more secure, knowing that even after Monica and Jay passed away, Olivia's income would increase to 75% of Monica's benefit—approximately $1,650/month.

> **NOTE:** SSI opens the door. DAC secures the future. Plan early so your child doesn't fall through the cracks.

How DAC Opens the Door to Medicare Eligibility

Medicare becomes available to individuals receiving SSDI or DAC after a 24-month waiting period. This is significant for individuals with disabilities who may age out of pediatric Medicaid programs or face coverage gaps as adults. Having both Medicaid and Medicare can expand access to providers and reduce out-of-pocket costs.

Being dually eligible for Medicare and Medicaid provides broader coverage. Medicare may cover doctor visits and hospital care, under a wider net of providers than Medicaid. Medicaid can cover long-term supports and services, like personal care aides and long-term care facilities.

> **NOTE:** DAC opens the door to Medicare, which in turn expands access to care. Don't overlook this milestone—it can change everything.

Work Incentives: Earning Without Losing Support

One of the biggest fears families express is: "If my loved one works, will they lose their benefits?" Thankfully, the answer is not necessarily. The Social Security Administration has several **work incentive programs** that allow individuals with disabilities to work while still keeping some or all of their benefits—at least for a transition period.

These programs are designed to encourage independence and support individuals as they test their ability to work. Here are a few key available programs:

- **Trial Work Period (TWP):** For SSDI or DAC recipients, this allows them to work for 9 months (within a rolling 60-month window) while still receiving full benefits, no matter how much they earn.
- **Extended Period of Eligibility (EPE):** After the trial period, individuals still have 36 months during which they can receive benefits for any month their earnings fall below a certain threshold (Substantial Gainful Activity, or SGA).
- **Ticket to Work:** A free, voluntary program connecting beneficiaries with employment services and job coaching.

- **Impairment-related Work Expenses (IRWE):** Costs for things like transportation, assistive tech, or job coaching may be deducted from gross income when determining eligibility.
- **SSI Earned Income Exclusion:** For SSI recipients, not all earned income counts against benefits. SSA excludes the first $65 of earned income and half of the rest when calculating monthly SSI reductions.

Benefits aren't an all-or-nothing deal. With work incentives, your child can earn a paycheck and keep the safety net.

NAVIGATING GOVERNMENT BENEFITS WITH CONFIDENCE

Government benefits aren't just support systems—they're essential building blocks in a long-term plan to support your loved one's autonomy and supported independence. From Medicaid waivers that open the door to community-based services, to SSI and DAC benefits that provide monthly income and health coverage, these programs offer more than financial assistance—they offer opportunity and stability.

But understanding these benefits, and how they intersect, is no easy task. Rules vary by state. Timing matters. Documentation is key. And persistence is often required. Whether it's applying for a waiver, securing SSI, transitioning to DAC, or navigating dual eligibility for Medicaid and Medicare, the process can feel overwhelming.

And yet, families do it every day. You have the guidance. You have the tools. Feel free to seek out an expert if you need help. You can do this!

Case Study: Putting It All Together

Meet Henry. He's 20 years old, has an intellectual disability, and lives at home with his mom, Angela. Angela is committed to building a secure future for Henry, but she's overwhelmed by the patchwork of programs, rules, and paperwork involved in planning.

At age 18, Angela applied for SSI on Henry's behalf. She gathered school evaluations, IEPs, a letter from his pediatrician, and documentation of household income. She also formalized a lease agreement for Henry to contribute a portion of his benefits to household expenses, allowing him to qualify for the full SSI benefit.

With that approval came automatic Medicaid eligibility in their state. Angela used the time between ages 18 and 22 to apply for a Medicaid waiver—Henry was placed on a waitlist but eventually qualified for a program that provided a personal care aide, day programming, and respite for Angela. These supports allowed Angela to return to part-time work.

At 21, Henry started part-time work at a local library with the help of a job coach. Through SSA's work incentive programs, he was able to earn wages without immediately losing benefits. Angela monitored his income and reported it monthly to SSA.

At age 23, Angela's husband (Henry's dad) retired. Henry now qualified for DAC benefits based on his father's work record. His new benefit was higher than his SSI amount, and he transitioned off SSI while maintaining Medicaid due to his previously established status. Two years later, Henry became eligible for Medicare, gaining broader access to medical providers.

Today, Henry receives DAC, Medicaid, and Medicare. He works part-time, attends a day program, and has in-home support through his Medicaid waiver. Angela feels relief knowing she's built a stable foundation that will support Henry for decades to come.

> **NOTE:** Planning step by step pays off. Each benefit builds on the next to create a secure, supported future.

This chapter has given you a roadmap. Use it to take the next step and remember: each action builds on the last. Start early, stay informed, and don't be afraid to ask questions. These programs were created to help—and with the right plan, they absolutely can.

FINAL THOUGHTS

The most powerful thing we can give our loved ones is a stable foundation. Government benefits are a part of that—not the whole picture, but an essential piece. When families understand how these systems work, they can build plans that not only meet needs, but they empower lives. You've got this.

Chapter 7

Tax Flexibility and Strategy

Here's the hard truth: tax laws change frequently. What's true in 2025 may not be true in 2035. As special needs planners, we've seen how sudden legislative shifts—like the SECURE Act—can disrupt carefully laid estate plans. That's why we tell families: Don't try to future-proof your plan with predictions. Future-proof it with flexibility.

In this chapter, we'll explore how flexibility to your executor or trustee can provide the ability to make tax-efficient decisions (and how to give specific instructions while also providing that flexibility). We will also look at key tax rules that impact special needs families, including the SECURE Act and "Stretch IRAs." We will explore some legal concepts such as an Applicable Multi-beneficiary trust and why it matters.

All of these come together to give you some ideas to discuss with your CPA and attorney to make your estate as tax-efficient as possible.

Our biggest reminder: your estate documents should direct your fiduciaries to consult a special needs financial planner and attorney. Because the best tax strategy is a current one—and only experts can help interpret it in real time.

> **NOTE:** Tax laws shift. Make your plan flexible enough to shift with them.

THE PROBLEM: TAX COMPLEXITY THAT OUTPACES YOUR ESTATE PLAN

Most estate plans are designed around today's laws. But your child may need support for 30, 40, even 50 years after your death. If your documents are rigid, your family could miss out on major tax advantages—or worse, pay unnecessary taxes that erode the legacy you intended.

There is also a trend in the legal landscape to give attorneys—and individuals and families—more flexibility within their estate plans to make future changes—even in irrevocable trusts. While the intent of an irrevocable trust cannot change, with the right language they can be amended to provide flexibility to adapt to current laws, even and especially tax laws.

The solution? Build documents that empower your executor or trustee to make tax-savvy decisions at the time of your death, not years (or decades) earlier when the documents were signed. That means including language that allows for tax-efficient disclaimers, asset allocation flexibility, and requires consultation with tax, legal, and financial special needs professionals. It's not about having a crystal ball—it's about having a flexible framework.

STRETCH IRAs AND THE SECURE ACT: WHAT CHANGED

Before the SECURE Act passed in 2019, many beneficiaries of inherited IRAs could "stretch" the required minimum distributions (RMDs) over their lifetime. This minimized annual taxes and allowed the funds to grow.

The SECURE Act changed all that. Now, most beneficiaries must withdraw the full balance within 10 years of the original account holder's death. That means higher taxes in a shorter window—and fewer growth opportunities.

However, there are exceptions. One of the most important exceptions is for individuals with disabilities. If your child qualifies as a disabled beneficiary under IRS rules, a properly structured Special Needs Trust can still take advantage of the lifetime "stretch" distribution schedule.

This makes the trust document's language—and its classification—as important as the investment itself. We cannot stress enough that having an attorney that understands this language—and will either include language specific to the Secure Act or provide clauses that give the trustee the ability to amend the trust to current tax laws—is crucial when retirement benefits are involved.

APPLICABLE MULTI-BENEFICIARY TRUSTS (AMBTs)

When planning for a loved one with a disability, your trust may name multiple beneficiaries—including the disabled individual and, eventually, siblings or other heirs. This creates a complication: many trusts with multiple beneficiaries lose the ability to "stretch" inherited retirement accounts.

Remainder beneficiaries—those who inherit after the primary (often disabled) beneficiary—are often siblings or extended family. But their existence affects the structure of the trust and how it's taxed.

If your goal is to preserve stretch provisions or minimize tax burdens, your trust needs to follow certain guidelines. Consulting with an elder law attorney to see if these provisions apply to you is critical. These provisions may include the following:

- Define the disabled beneficiary as the only primary lifetime beneficiary
- Clearly state the terms for distributing assets to remainder beneficiaries
- Use the correct trust classification (like AMBT)

Remainder beneficiaries may inherit sizable sums—but how and when they inherit can impact how the entire trust is taxed. Enter the AMBT. This type of trust is designed to preserve lifetime stretch treatment for the disabled beneficiary, while still providing for remainder beneficiaries after their death.

There are two important requirements. The disabled individual must be the sole current beneficiary during their lifetime. The other beneficiaries can only inherit after their death. This is important. We have seen trusts structured as "sprinkling trusts" that provide income to multiple beneficiaries at the same time. This will not qualify under the Secure Act and will not allow you to preserve the stretch benefit for your loved one.

We have consulted with many attorneys on the ins and outs of an AMBT and the Secure Act. Some have learned the intricacies and details inside and out. Most tell us that it is better to use broader, flexible language instructing the trustee to seek advice at the time the estate is settled and amend according to current rules.

> **NOTE:** While it's always beneficial to stay up to date on current laws, flexible language can make sure your loved one receives advice specific to their needs, at the time that they need it.

ROTH CONVERSIONS: A POWERFUL TOOL—SOMETIMES

A Roth conversion means taking money from a traditional IRA or 401(k), paying taxes on it now, and moving it into a Roth IRA where it grows tax-free. We hear a lot of different opinions on whether the Roth conversion makes sense for special needs families. After all, if higher income parents are leaving money to a low-income disabled dependent—it seems to make sense to pass the tax liability to them.

The answer is much more complicated. While the disabled dependent may be in a much lower income bracket, they may not be in a position to receive all the income. And if the income has to stay inside the special needs trust, it could be taxed at the highest tax bracket (more on that later in this chapter). Taxes could be the largest detractor to making sure a special needs trust covers the funding your child needs over their lifetime—and there are steps you can take to reduce those taxes for them. Roth IRA conversions could be one of them.

Some of the benefits of a Roth IRA are about more than just taxes. A trustee does not have to worry about Required Minimum Distributions or engage in lengthy annual tax planning/strategy.

And the tax reasons are really more than enough. The tax-free growth inside the Roth IRA means that the trust isn't paying taxes on the growth of the asset—nor is it paying tax when the money is coming out. The trustee doesn't have to worry about which source of income it distributed out to the trustee when filing taxes. And overall, the trust can avoid the compressed tax brackets.

We believe that Roth IRAs are one of the most powerful financial tools available when funding a special needs trust. From both a tax perspective and a long-term growth standpoint, Roth IRAs offer unmatched benefits. Tax-free withdrawals mean the trust can use the money without generating taxable income for the trust or the beneficiary. And since Roth IRAs are not subject to required minimum distributions, the trustee has greater control over timing and distributions. The value of tax-free compound growth over decades can be substantial—especially in a multi-generational plan.

Here's the real impact: We sometimes ask parents to accept a short-term tax hit today—by doing strategic Roth conversions during retirement or in low-income years—so their child isn't burdened with compressed trust taxes and inflexible income rules later. That tax "pain" now can translate to decades of financial freedom for their child.

Case Study: Roth Conversion

For example, Mike and Elena, parents of 22-year-old Jordan, who has a developmental disability, worked with a planner to gradually convert $400,000 from Mike's traditional IRA to a Roth over 15 years. While it meant paying extra taxes during those years, they knew their son's special needs trust would ultimately inherit a fully tax-free account. Fast forward to today, that Roth IRA has grown significantly—allowing

Jordan's trust to fund therapies, social activities, and housing supports without worrying about annual tax burdens in the future.

> **NOTE:** IRS Publication 590-B (Distributions from IRAs), SECURE Act of 2019, and follow-up legislation under the SECURE 2.0 Act of 2022 clarify Roth treatment and beneficiary rules.

But a Roth conversion isn't always wise. You must weigh all the factors in making the decision to do it. Take a look at your current income tax bracket, the size of the IRA, and the timing (spreading conversions over multiple years).

Sometimes, families experience lower income between when they retire officially from their jobs, and when they file for Social Security and start taking distributions from taxable retirement accounts. Or they experience increasing medical costs as they age due to paying for long-term care and other expenses. Both of these can provide opportunities for additional Roth IRA conversions. Keeping an eye on your annual income, tax bracket, and more will help you determine if doing a Roth conversion is right for your family.

In summary, Roth conversion can make your estate more tax-efficient—but only with careful planning and expert guidance.

Checklist: When to Consider a Roth Conversion

You should consider a Roth conversion in these cases:

- You're in a temporarily lower income tax bracket (e.g., early retirement years)
- You're not yet receiving Social Security or pension income

- You expect future tax rates to increase
- You want to reduce taxable Required Minimum Distributions (RMDs)
- You have high anticipated medical expenses (which may offset taxable income)
- You plan to leave assets to a Special Needs Trust or other long-term legacy vehicle
- You have the funds available to pay conversion taxes without drawing from the IRA
- You are actively coordinating your estate with a special needs financial planner or CPA

> **TIP:** Consider scheduling annual reviews to evaluate whether partial Roth conversions make sense based on your tax return and current estate strategy.

THE COSTLY MISTAKES OF TAX STRATEGIES

Even well-intentioned families can make costly mistakes when tax strategies are poorly implemented or misunderstood. Here are two real-world examples.

The Nonprofit Remainder Beneficiary Mishap

Carol left her $850,000 IRA to a Special Needs Trust for her son, Ethan, who has autism. She wanted any leftover funds to benefit her favorite nonprofit. Unfortunately, the trust didn't include specific language regarding tax treatment or how to handle charitable remainder beneficiaries. Because the trust included a nonindividual (the nonprofit) as a remainder beneficiary, it failed to qualify as an AMBT. The result? The entire IRA had to be distributed—and taxed—within five years rather than over Ethan's lifetime. What could have provided decades of tax deferred growth became fully taxable in less than five years, paying the highest tax bracket in each of those five years.

Missing Tax Guidance in the Trust

Paul's parents left him a well-structured trust—but it lacked clear language directing the trustee to consult with tax and financial professionals and allowing them to make necessary changes. When Paul's trustee inherited a traditional IRA, they didn't realize that the trust's structure meant the IRA withdrawals were taxed at trust rates—often 37% or higher. Had they consulted a planner or implemented a Roth conversion earlier, hundreds of thousands of dollars could have been preserved for Paul's support.

> **NOTE:** The lesson here is that the right language—and the right professionals—can protect decades of care.

WHY WE RECOMMEND A SEPARATE TAX ID FOR SPECIAL NEEDS TRUSTS

There is debate among attorneys and planners about whether a Special Needs Trust should use the Social Security Number (SSN) of the beneficiary or obtain its own Employer Identification Number (EIN).

Here's our position: we recommend getting a separate Tax ID (EIN) for the trust. Why? We believe it is the best way to provide a clear legal and financial firewall between the individual and the assets. It keeps the trust's income completely separate from the beneficiary's. And it avoids confusion in government reporting and benefit eligibility.

Technically, you shouldn't have to do this—legally, the trust income is supposed to be separate and not impacting benefits eligibility—even when reported on the beneficiary's tax return. However, we've consulted with multiple attorneys who have seen cases challenged in court—cases where a trust using the beneficiary's Social Security number raised red flags. Those attorneys agree: the best protection is a standalone tax identity.

> **NOTE:** Avoid gray areas. A separate tax ID gives your trust clear legal standing and avoids costly mistakes.

Now you might be asking why it matters if you use a separate tax ID for special needs trusts or not. The reason is the taxation of trusts. A trust with its own tax ID is considered its own separate entity, subject to a compressed tax bracket. In plain language, this means the trust pays tax at a higher rate on lower amounts of income. Using a separate tax ID means your trust will pay at those higher tax rates—and is part of why we think tax efficiency in investments inside the trust is so important.

GRANTOR TRUSTS IN SPECIAL NEEDS PLANNING

Another aspect of tax planning within the special needs trust world is use of the grantor trust. This gets back to the idea of when you plan to fund the trust. If you plan to fund the trust after you pass away, or at your death, then grantor trust status is not needed. However, if you plan to fund the trust while one or both spouses are still alive, you may consider a grantor trust.

The grantor trust status allows the assets inside the trust to be taxed at the grantor's tax rates and on their tax return—with the grantor being the person who funded the trust. Typically, parents are the grantors and would be taxed at lower rates than the trust itself. This is another area where consultation with an estate planning attorney, a CPA, and a special needs planner is helpful.

Grandparents might use a grantor trust to put assets in before they pass away, to help their kids defray the cost of providing for their special needs grandchild. Parents might choose to put a home, a car, or other asset that is intended only for the use of their child inside the trust.

It's important to know that grantor trust status is only valid while the grantor is alive. Once they pass away, the trust becomes an irrevocable special needs trust and will need to use either the beneficiary's Social Security number or obtain a tax ID of its own.

In general, we recommend waiting until the death of the parents to fund a special needs trust—but there are still many exceptions to that generality, and it always depends on the needs of the family.

FINAL THOUGHTS

Your estate doesn't need to predict future tax law—it needs to adapt to it. That's why trusts must be written with flexibility. It's why we encourage documents to empower executors and trustees to seek advice and why tax treatment must be optimized not just for today, but for decades. You could be using that trust tomorrow—or in 50 years.

At the end of the day, you are creating a plan not just for transfer of wealth but for transfer of care, security, and dignity. Make sure it's protected.

> **NOTE:** Recommended Language in Estate Documents that attorneys we work with have used: "The Trustee is directed to seek guidance from a qualified special needs financial planner or tax advisor upon the death of the Grantor, to determine the most tax-efficient method for distributing and managing all assets held within the trust." Feel free to run this language by your attorney, to see if this would work for your family.

The laws may change. Your child's needs may not. Make your plan flexible enough to adapt, and strong enough to protect.

Chapter 8

Insurance: Protecting the Future with Confidence

"We've done everything we were supposed to," Adam tells us, worry in his voice. "Sabrina has her services, her supports, her community—but what happens when we're gone?"

Their story is like so many families we meet. They've built a strong foundation: IEPs, waiver services, SSI applications, and daily joy-filled routines. But there's one thing they can't see clearly: the future.

From weekend Starbucks trips to annual Disney vacations, the extras that make Sabrina's life joyful are at risk if Adam and Teresa are no longer here to fund them. Sabrina's SSI benefit—currently about $943/month—covers the basics but not the life they envisioned for her. And their own retirement savings are just that—enough to cover their lifetime, but not enough for Sabrina.

So, what's the plan? Insurance might be the answer.

WHAT IS INSURANCE?

Insurance is a financial tool that helps manage risk. When you purchase insurance, you're essentially entering into a contract with an insurance company: you pay a premium (or monthly fee), and in return, they promise to provide a payout if a certain event occurs—like death, disability, or long-term care needs.

There are many types of insurance, but in special needs planning, we focus most often on life insurance, disability insurance, and long-term care insurance.

Let's start by doing a deep dive on the different types of life insurance:

- **Group Term Life Insurance:** Often provided through an employer, this coverage is usually limited to one to two times your salary and only lasts as long as you're employed. It's convenient but not portable.
- **Term Life Insurance:** Provides coverage for a set number of years (e.g., 10, 20, or 30 years). It's affordable and ideal for replacing income during your working years.
- **Convertible Term Life Insurance:** This is term insurance with a key benefit—you can convert it into permanent insurance later, without a medical exam.
- **Whole Life Insurance:** Permanent insurance that builds cash value. Premiums are higher, but coverage lasts for life and includes a savings component.

- **Universal Life Insurance:** A flexible type of permanent insurance where you can adjust premiums and death benefits over time.
- **Survivorship Life Insurance:** Covers two people (usually spouses) and pays out only after both have passed away. It's often used to fund a special needs trust. Survivorship life insurance is typically less expensive than individual policies on each parent, especially when one parent has a preexisting condition or lower insurance rating. This type of insurance makes sense when the financial need arises not upon the first death—but when both parents are gone and their dependent child is left needing financial support. It's a permanent policy, meaning it doesn't expire as long as premiums are paid, and it can be a powerful tool to create stability for a child with lifelong needs. Because it insures two lives instead of one, the insurance company assumes less risk, which often results in lower premiums. It's also an excellent solution when only one spouse is insurable or when cost is a major consideration.

> **Caution:** Some agents may recommend overfunded or cash-value life insurance (like whole life or indexed universal life) as an "investment vehicle." While these can work for high-net-worth families, they are often overkill for families simply trying to fund a special needs trust. If you just need the death benefit, term or survivorship policies are more cost-effective. Don't let a sales pitch steer your plan off course. Whole life insurance may be the right choice, but make sure you know what the goal is for your insurance and what you need it to do. Overfunded life insurance may have the goal of providing *you* tax-free income in your retirement, which is not the usual goal for life insurance in special needs planning.

LIFE INSURANCE TO FUND THE COST OF CARE

Let's go back to Adam and Teresa. Since Sabrina has the Medicaid waiver, her housing, food, monitoring, and medical expenses are mostly paid for. But she has hippotherapy that she loves, a weekly outing to a golf course that is important to her (she's an avid golfer), and some social activities that are important to her. Here is a summary:

Monthly Expenses	$800
Annual Cost	$9,600
Lifetime Projection (Ages 21–92)	**$691,848**

Sabrina's needs don't end when school ends. In Teresa and Adam's case, this is where the cost-of-care assessment that we mentioned in Chapter 4 connects directly to an insurance plan. You know what you need to fund. And you have looked at all alternatives. Insurance becomes the best tool to create that funding.

Life insurance has many benefits. For one, it can act as a permission slip: giving the parents permission to spend their retirement savings on themselves. It can also be a multiplier—taking a small amount of money and making it into a larger amount of money, without taking market risk. It provides a source of tax-free assets to the trust. The funding itself can offer a buffer if government benefits are reduced, interrupted, or lost due to political or administrative changes.

For Adam and Teresa, their retirement was mostly covered by Adam's pension and Teresa's Social Security. They were not high wage earners, and much of their extra funding was spent on therapies for Teresa that were not covered by her waiver. That meant that life insurance was their best bet at providing her the money she would need to cover her lifetime cost of care.

WHEN TO USE CONVERTIBLE TERM

During your working years, term insurance is often the most cost-effective way to protect against lost income, liabilities, and future needs like the cost of care or college expenses. The face amount is typically large, which provides valuable leverage.

What does convertible term, or the option to convert to permanent, really mean? This option gives you the right to purchase permanent insurance later—without going through medical underwriting. Many insurance companies offer the option to convert to permanent in small chunks, meaning that you have more control over your budget and can purchase permanent insurance as your income and savings go up.

A well-structured term policy should also include the option to convert to permanent insurance later—either to fund long-term care or a survivorship need. The reason this is important is that we see many families who wait to purchase permanent insurance until they are older and really need it. Now they have the need, they apply—but due to health reasons, they are uninsurable. There are a myriad of reasons you might be uninsurable—a mental health diagnosis, a diabetes diagnosis, an autoimmune disease. You may be able to maintain it well, but underwriting may still decline you for insurance.

Applying while you are young and healthy—and purchasing term insurance with the option to convert later—allows you to take advantage of your health now, pay lower premiums while you are younger, and then decide when you are older if you want or need to convert to permanent insurance. Best-case scenarios—either you don't need the insurance, or you don't need to use the option to convert because you are still healthy and can go through traditional underwriting. But in the case that you have a new diagnosis or health condition that has come up, you have given yourself the option to purchase permanent insurance.

Careful: many inexpensive online term policies do not allow conversion. If you're planning long term, make sure your policy gives you options. Without the option to convert, your health may change, you may receive a new diagnosis, which would make you ineligible for a new insurance policy. For special needs families, we must think of that future need and leave the option open.

Now what happens if you already have a chronic health condition or have recently had an injury or illness that you are worried will make you uninsurable? We always say, collect the data so that you know what you are dealing with. Instead of making a decision (or simply not taking action) because of fear, call your special needs planner and have an open discussion with them. Licensed insurance agents can find out if your condition will allow you to be underwritten to receive insurance. They can also shop around to see if there is a company who would be okay underwriting you. You may end up paying more—but it doesn't mean the door is completely closed to you. Have the conversation and know what your options are.

And if you are not insurable, have that conversation with your agent as well. Make sure the rest of your plan is rock solid. And do the best you can with the funds that you have. Information helps us make informed decisions—and can help us guide our future behavior. It may mean adjusting your retirement budget to include higher savings. Or looking outside of your immediate family to see if there is another family member that could purchase life insurance or fund the trust from other sources. Make sure you are looking at all of your options. It takes planning—and a village—to care for a disabled individual. We are all in this together.

CASE STUDY: THE MORRIS FAMILY

Julia and Marcus Morris purchased a 30-year convertible term policy when they were in their early 30s and had just had their second child, Daniel, who has a rare genetic disorder. They knew their income was tight, but they needed a large face amount in case either of them passed away prematurely.

As they approached their early 60s, the term policy was nearing expiration. With retirement on the horizon and their savings modest, they worked with a special needs planner to convert their term policy into a survivorship policy. This new policy would ensure a tax-free payout to Daniel's trust once both parents had passed—providing lifelong stability for their son without them needing to purchase new insurance at older ages or go through medical underwriting.

This two-phase strategy allowed the Morrises to afford protection during their working years and secure permanent coverage for their son's future.

Many Purposes of Life Insurance

Funding a special needs trust is an incredibly important use for life insurance proceeds. When looking at your family's financial plan, there may be other gaps or risks that need to be addressed. The fact is that special needs families have higher needs for income—which means that things like disability or premature death of a wage earner or caregiver in the household can affect our families in disproportionately larger ways. And social safety nets don't kick in for families until income and assets fall under certain (very low) limits, leaving the family to live in poverty.

Making sure that a calculation is done for things like income replacement, paying off a mortgage, and leaving money for larger planned expenses such as college is important. This is another reason we call it multigenerational planning. In the following example of the Morris family, we will take a look at how they used life insurance to fund their care.

Morris Family Insurance Snapshot

Marcus and Julia Morris were 49 and 45 years old. Marcus was earning $15,000/month at his job while Julia was a stay-at-home caregiver of their daughter Louisa. Louisa had complex medical needs and was often hospitalized. At age 13, she had spent much of her young life in and out of the hospital and struggled to keep up with schoolwork and socialization—though those were two activities she really enjoyed. Their monthly household expenses were $10,000/month, which included $2,000/month they received for caregiving from Medicaid for Louisa.

They calculated a lifetime cost of care for Louisa at $1.5 million and realized that they had nowhere near enough saved to cover that amount for her. As they crunched numbers, they realized that life insurance needed to be a part of the solution. Table 8.1 shows a breakdown of the different factors they took into account when deciding how much insurance to purchase and what types of purchase they needed: first, income

Table 8.1 Factors to Consider in Purchasing Insurance

Need	Amount to Cover	Insurance Type	Why This Works
Income Replacement	$15,000/month (gross)	30-year Convertible Term	Provides high coverage while the wage earner is working. Convertible to permanent later.
Caregiver Replacement	$5,000/month	30-year Convertible Term	Provides coverage to pay for caregiving support while other parent is working.
Cost of Care for Daughter	$1.5 million (lifetime)	Survivorship Life Insurance (converted from term)	Pays out at second death, funds special needs trust. More affordable than individual policies.
Disability Coverage	60–70% of income	Private Long-term Disability Insurance with own-occupation rider	Replaces income if primary earner becomes disabled.
Long-term Care (for parents)	$200/day or more in later years	Rider on Permanent Life Policy or stand-alone LTC	Protects retirement assets if care is needed.

replacement in case Marcus passed away. And please—don't forget the value of your caregiver. While they may not be paid to do the work, if they were not there, someone would need to be paid to do it. And as parent, you are probably wearing many different hats. Take those all into account when calculating your number and deciding how to pay for insurance and what products you need.

Marcus also went back to his work and maximized his disability insurance to cover 60% of his wages in case he was disabled. He knew that it did not provide him with transferrable coverage, but it fit in their budget and allowed him to maximize coverage while spending more on the life insurance—which him and Julia felt was a larger risk.

They purchased $2.5 million of convertible term today on Marcus, and $2 million of convertible term on Julia, with the idea that they could purchase a survivorship policy and long-term care insurance later. They purchased what was within their budget and covered their risk in a thoughtful way—not every risk, but a level they felt comfortable with.

WHAT SURVIVORSHIP INSURANCE IS

Survivorship life insurance, also known as second-to-die insurance, is a type of permanent life insurance that covers two individuals (usually spouses) and pays a death benefit only after the second insured person has passed away.

This strategy is particularly useful in special needs planning because it ensures funding is available at the time it is most needed—when both caregivers are gone. It is typically more affordable than purchasing two separate permanent policies. Survivorship may also be easier to obtain—particularly if there is a large age gap between spouses, or one spouse does not qualify on their own/is rated poorly due to health concerns.

The death benefit from a survivorship policy is commonly directed to a special needs trust, ensuring that the child continues to receive supplemental financial support for their lifetime, without jeopardizing eligibility for government benefits.

This is not short-term planning—this is long-term legacy planning. Survivorship life insurance is a way to provide for your child with confidence, knowing that even after you're gone, their life can continue with security and flexibility

As we said before, there is another benefit to life insurance: when life insurance covers the child's entire cost of care, it can act as a permission slip to the parents to spend their hard-earned retirement savings on themselves without worrying about their child's well-being after they're gone.

USING AN IRREVOCABLE LIFE INSURANCE TRUST

In some cases, families choose to own life insurance through an irrevocable life insurance trust (ILIT). An ILIT is a separate legal entity designed specifically to own a life insurance policy and remove it from the insured person's taxable estate. Why does this matter?

If the value of your estate—including life insurance proceeds—exceeds federal or state estate tax thresholds, your heirs could lose a significant portion to taxes. By having the policy owned by an ILIT, the proceeds avoid estate taxation altogether, preserving the full value for the beneficiaries.

This is especially important for families with large estates, real estate or business holdings, and/or a desire to leave a sizable inheritance and avoiding any future change in state tax laws.

An ILIT can also provide structure and control. It names a trustee to manage the assets, outlines how funds should be distributed, and protects the inheritance from creditors or mismanagement. Essentially, the ILIT owns the insurance policy—not the insured(s), and the entity is completely separate from the insureds estate. Parents (or sometimes, grandparents) would still pay the premiums for the life insurance. The proceeds would then be directed to the special needs trust.

For special needs families, a carefully drafted special needs trust can sometimes serve dual purposes—acting as both a special needs trust and an ILIT if set up correctly. This allows families to fund the trust with insurance proceeds, avoid estate taxes, and ensure funds are managed according to their wishes.

However, ILITs are irrevocable—you can't change your mind once it's created—so it's important to work with an attorney and planner who understand how to coordinate these strategies with your overall estate and care planning.

An ILIT requires careful planning—and should be done in consultation with an attorney, a special needs financial planner, and a CPA.

LONG-TERM CARE INSURANCE: PLANNING FOR PARENTAL NEEDS

Long-term care insurance helps cover the cost of services that support individuals with chronic health conditions who need assistance with activities of daily living, such as bathing, dressing, and eating.

This is important in special needs planning because parents are often the primary caregivers, and if they require long-term care themselves, it could have unintended consequences. Financial resources could be directed to the parents and away from their child's future. Caregiving roles could be disrupted. And it could create an unexpected financial and caregiving burden on siblings.

We also encourage you to speak to your own parents about their planning and especially what they will do as they age with their long-term care needs. We see more and more caregivers as part of the sandwich generation: caring for aging parents, while also caring for their special needs children. Being able to plan appropriately—and help grandparents set-up appropriate plans—can take stress off everyone involved.

Long-term care insurance has many benefits. It may provide a source of dedicated funds to pay for home health aides, assisted living, or nursing care. Both spouses and children can have peace of mind that one spouse won't deplete shared resources if the other requires extended care. And these days, many policies give the option to age at home longer (age in place), with paid help. The current trend is to keep people out of facilities and at home for as long as possible.

Consider starting a policy in your late 40s to early 60s, when premiums are still relatively affordable and health underwriting is more favorable. Many permanent life insurance policies can include a long-term care rider, or some families may consider stand-alone long-term care policies. Be sure to also ask the question and make sure you understand how the policy pays for the long-term care. Some send you a check once you have qualified to be used however you see fit and to defray costs. Others need you to send receipts and seek reimbursement. The latter is more common; the former can be less stressful.

Long-term care insurance is another way to protect your family's financial plan and caregiving structure from unexpected health events and stress on your multigenerational plan.

DISABILITY INSURANCE: A CRITICAL PIECE OF THE PUZZLE

Disability insurance is often overlooked in financial planning, but for special needs families, it's essential. It protects your ability to earn an income—the very foundation of your financial plan.

There are two primary types:

- **Short-term disability** covers a portion of your income for a few weeks to months after injury or illness.
- **Long-term disability** provides income replacement if you cannot work for an extended period due to a serious medical condition.

Many employers offer group disability policies, and these typically cover 40–60% of your income. Group policies are more cost-effective—but they are often not portable and more limited in scope. That means if you change jobs or stop working, you lose coverage—and getting a new policy later may require medical underwriting or come with exclusions.

Private disability insurance offers more flexibility. You can tailor coverage amounts, ensure the benefit is tax-free, and choose an **own-occupation rider**, which means you qualify for benefits if you can't perform your specific job—even if you could do something else. Be sure to call your employer if disability insurance is offered and understand what benefits the plan offers. Some will still offer an own occupation rider.

Some disability policies also allow you to continue contributing to retirement savings plans like a 401(k) while on claim, ensuring your future is still protected.

The bottom line is that if you're a primary wage earner or caregiver in a special needs household, disability insurance isn't optional—it's foundational. You want to make sure you have some form of it while in your working years.

HOW TO CHOOSE THE RIGHT INSURANCE PLAN: A FAMILY FRAMEWORK

When deciding how much and what type of insurance you need, consider the following framework:

1. Assess your needs:
    - What are your monthly expenses?
    - How much income needs to be replaced if one parent can't work or passes away?
    - What's the lifetime cost of care for your loved one?
    - What's the cost of caregiving that you either currently pay for or are doing unpaid?
2. Understand the tools available:
    - Term for income replacement
    - Convertible term for flexibility
    - Survivorship for legacy planning
    - Disability insurance for income protection
    - Long-term care insurance to protect parental care and resources
    - ILITs for estate planning and tax efficiency

3. Ask these questions when meeting with an insurance agent or special needs planner:
   - Is this policy portable if I change jobs?
   - Can I convert this policy later without medical underwriting?
   - What happens if I become disabled—can I continue premium payments?
   - Does the policy offer riders that are relevant to our situation (e.g., own-occupation, waiver of premium)?
   - Is this policy owned inside a trust or my estate—and what are the tax consequences?
4. Reevaluate at major life milestones:
   - Birth of a child
   - Diagnosis
   - Change in income
   - Retirement planning

With the right questions and a clear understanding of your goals, insurance can go from being a product to a powerful planning tool—helping you protect what matters most.

FINAL THOUGHTS

Insurance isn't just about risk management—it's about peace of mind. In special needs planning, insurance becomes a bridge between what you have and what your loved one will need in the future. It fills in the financial gaps that government benefits and savings alone cannot cover. It protects your family from the unpredictable—illness, income loss, long-term care needs—and ensures that your child's quality of life continues, even when you're no longer here. Insurance gives parents the confidence to enjoy their own retirement, knowing that their child will be cared for. It creates security, flexibility, and a legacy of love.

Chapter 9

Estate Planning Strategies and Concepts

This chapter was written by Penelope Gaffney, attorney at Gravis Law, in collaboration with Kristin, Kathy, and Mary

Many hear the terms *estate planning* and think it is a concept reserved for families with significant wealth or means. This misconception can result in families putting off the process or avoiding it entirely. This chapter explains what estate planning is and why it is an important consideration for every family.

CASE STUDY: MEET THE SINGHS

Priya and Amar Singh are the parents of three children—Neel, age 24; Maya, age 21; and Arjun, age 16. Neel has autism and, while highly verbal and intellectually gifted, requires daily support for certain executive tasks and does not live independently. Maya is a college student pursuing a career in environmental science. Arjun, the youngest, is in high school and actively involved in sports.

As the Singhs began planning their estate, they felt overwhelmed. Their assets weren't vast, but their responsibilities were. How could they ensure that Neel would be supported throughout his lifetime, without causing feelings of resentment from Maya and Arjun? They wanted to be fair—but what does fairness look like? And, if something were to happen to the parents before Arjun finished high school, who would be his guardian?

These questions are the very topics estate planning addresses.

WHAT IS ESTATE PLANNING?

Estate planning is the process of arranging how your assets will be managed and distributed after your death. This includes planning for your medical and financial affairs, if you are no longer able to make those decisions by yourself. For special needs families, this also usually includes considering what role trusts should play in supporting and protecting every member of your family. Estate planning can ensure a disabled member receives the care and support they need, without jeopardizing their access to important government benefits such as Social Security and Medicaid. For this reason, it is important to talk with a qualified attorney to determine what is most appropriate for your family.

Typically, an estate plan will have Wills, Trusts and/or Special Needs Trusts, Power of Attorney documents, a Letter of Intent, and in many cases, a microboard. Let's break that down in the following sections.

Wills: Informing Others of Your Wishes

A will, also referred to as a Last Will and Testament, is a document representing the wishes of one person, who is called the Testator. It specifies how their assets and property should be distributed after their death, who will serve as the guardian for their minor children, and who will manage the estate, termed an Executor, Personal Representative, or Administrator. A will can address several items, such as personal property and tangible items, and it typically nominates successor or alternative administrators as well as family members or beneficiaries. To be legally valid, it must be in writing, signed by the testator, and witnessed.

A Living Will provides directions as to how your medical care should be handled, such as whether you want to be resuscitated, intubated, be given palliative care, or any other wishes you have.

Trusts: Establishing an Entity for Your Assets

Trusts are created to manage assets and to control how they are distributed. The grantor is the person establishing the trust. The trustee is the person administering the trust or managing the trust assets, and the beneficiary is the person identified in the trust to receive a distribution, whether directly or on their behalf. Trusts can hold assets for short or long periods. They can have specific instructions on how and/or by who the money can be spent. It can specify the wishes of the grantor and provide the trustee with broad or limited discretion. The trustee must act as a fiduciary to the trust—meaning it must follow the specific instructions given in the trust.

Special Needs Trusts: Protecting and Supporting Individuals with Disabilities

Special needs trusts, also termed supplemental needs trusts, are designed to receive assets for the benefit of an individual who receives needs-based benefits. The assets are never deeded or titled in the name of the individual and the individual has no authority to demand how the assets are managed or when distributions are made.

The trustee, in their sole decision-making authority, can pay for the expenses of a disabled beneficiary that are not covered by public benefits, to support or improve their quality of life. They are established as an entity so that funds and assets can be held there on their behalf, without going to them directly.

This is important because public benefits require the disabled member to maintain eligibility for public benefits by limiting their assets, which means any direct inheritance or asset could jeopardize their ability to continually meet the public benefit resource limits. And since disabilities usually require some level of regular care, the costs to meet that level of care for a lifetime often exceed what most people can generally afford.

For example, if Josh is on public benefits, which cover the cost of his group home and day support program, and his mother passes and leaves him an inheritance of $10,000, it would exceed the $2,000 asset limit required by Medicaid (which funds his group home and day support), thus disqualifying him for the public benefits program. This means that Josh would lose access to his group home and day support programs. And since the average monthly cost of a group home is $4,000 and the average monthly cost of a day support program is $3,500, the inherited funds would only last a little over a month.

Even if we made it a larger amount such as $100,000, at the end of the day the cost to running these programs is significant and the services they provide are tremendously helpful. But, at the rate of the costs, few individuals can afford to pay on their own.

Power of Attorney Designations: Securing Help When You Most Need It

A power of attorney (POA) document designates authority to another person, termed the agent, to act on the behalf of an individual, the principal. POAs can act on behalf of the individual for financial and/or medical matters. It is recommended to establish a POA at age 18, for adults who can provide informed consent, to ensure someone has the authority to act on your behalf if you are incapacitated.

A durable power of attorney is a POA designation that is in effect for your lifetime, unless you revoke it or pass away. It can also include financial and medical matters. Importantly, a power of attorney ceases to have any authority after the death of the principal.

> **NOTE:** Decision-making support in the form of a power of attorney is something we recommend for *every* member of the family—because you never know when you will need that help or support.

Advance Medical Directives/Living Will: Sharing Your Dying Wishes

An advanced medical directive documents your wishes for medical care, including end-of-life treatment in case you are unable to communicate these wishes yourself.

With all these documents come a few considerations. First, legal documents are state specific. It is important to work with an attorney qualified to work in your state to ensure your documents meet state requirements and are filed appropriately, if necessary. The attorney can also help you navigate which documents make the most sense for you and your family.

ESTATE PLANNING IS MORE THAN "GETTING YOUR DOCUMENTS DONE"

Estate planning is protection. It is a process that gives information to those around you about how things are meant to be handled. In lieu of legal documents directing how your estate should be handled, the court will have to determine what to do with your assets. This is called probate. When you pass, probate is the process of the court reviewing your legal documents, confirming your executor, and proceeding with what you have put in place. In the absence of your documented plan, the probate process will have to take place and can be a long and challenging process for those you've left behind. Again, big or small, your estate must be handled, and as parents and caregivers of individuals with disabilities, it is important to do your estate planning early to ensure a clear pathway of protection and support for their lifetime.

Estate planning is also strategic. It allows you to determine which assets are best left to your loved ones. For example, it might be easiest and more straightforward to leave your life insurance policy to your loved one's special needs trust, while leaving more complicated assets such as retirement and investment accounts to others. Estate planning attorneys and financial advisors experienced in special needs planning can help you think through the best course of action.

HOW TO GET STARTED WITH ESTATE PLANNING

Estate planning is truly that, *planning!* This consists of thinking through your needs, the needs of your loved ones, and your assets. This is something you want to do, and early on, but it is important to take time to think through the best strategy that works for you and your family.

Think about your needs: taking time to consider how you would like your property and assets distributed is crucial. This is time you want to set aside and reflect on in a very intentional way.

Think about what needs to be in place. As parents and caregivers, we must consider what needs to be in place to support our loved one. This includes thinking about your loved one's cost of care, access to government benefits, and daily support. Consider this in advance and a qualified attorney can help you translate that into appropriate documents.

Consider the people in your life, what role should they play, or who should be named. Estate planning requires us to think about the people in our lives who we want to support and those that we need to help facilitate our plans. Consider your family members, friends, neighbors, and others who you may wish to leave something to and those that you think can help ensure what you have put together will be carried out.

We also encourage you to think through trustee roles, trust protectors, successors, and beneficiaries. It is important to work with your attorney to understand what the trustee will do, how they will do it, whether it makes sense to have trust protectors in place, and, of course, who will succeed those individuals if they are unable to serve at the time you need them to. Also, it is important to consider the beneficiaries, particularly in consideration of equitable distributions.

We cannot encourage the importance of this enough: you need to work with a qualified attorney. When working with an attorney, you will not only want to address the items listed here, but you will also want to make sure your legal documents address tax efficiency, regulations, and are written in a way that gives the grantor and trustee the flexibility to consult with experts and make adjustments, within the limits of the documents, but while meeting current standards.

Now you need to go back to your accounts and update your beneficiaries. Sometimes people go to all the trouble of establishing their estate plan but forget to go back and update their accounts. Even if you list a particular person in your will, if they are not also listed on the account, the account will trump what is written in the will. For example, if Bob wrote in his will that his new wife Sherry should receive his estate, yet he forgot to change the name on his retirement account from his first wife, Michelle, then the account will be distributed to Michelle at his death, not Sherry. Now certainly an attorney might be able to assist Michael in challenging that in court, but normally accounts must go to their listed beneficiaries, regardless of the will. Don't make that mistake!

> **NOTE:** Every few years (no longer than five), review your estate to make sure it still meets your needs.

AVOID COMMON MISTAKES

Estate planning is akin to strategy. It takes time and the help of experts. Be sure to give yourself that time and to access needed resources to put your plan into motion in the most effective way possible. Here are some common mistakes we see.

First, be realistic. If you intend to give your daughter your house as a "gift" to thank her for assisting with her brother's disability, that might backfire. Your daughter may not want to live in that house or go to the trouble of selling it. Maybe without you here, the house is no longer a good option for your son, given his care needs.

All this to say, every decision should be realistic and, better yet, discussed in advance with those involved. If you intend for your estate to help and support your loved ones, having intentional conversations while you are living is the best way to ensure that. We all know how uncomfortable the conversation is, but often as parents and caregivers, we've been in lots of uncomfortable situations, don't let this one get in the way.

This one is so important that say it multiple times: update your financial accounts. We just can't say this enough!

And last, informing people of your intentions is so important. Make sure the trustee you listed knows they are listed. Make sure the executor/personal representative in your will knows they have been designated. Make sure the successor trustees and executor/personal representative know as well. By letting them know in advance, they can prepare. Advance notice gives them the time to think through their questions so that they too feel supported and informed when the time comes.

THE IMPORTANCE OF EQUITABLE (NOT EQUAL) ESTATE PLANNING

The idea behind equitable planning is that fairness does not always mean equal distribution. As you consider the best way to handle your estate, consider every member of your family. Each child may have very different needs, levels of independence, and financial realities. An equal division of assets might appear neutral on paper, but it can result in vastly unfair outcomes—especially when one child has lifelong care needs and the others do not.

For the Singh family described earlier, this meant providing Neel with a special needs trust funded through life insurance and directing most other assets toward Maya and Arjun. They also documented their decisions in writing to explain their rationale and help prevent future conflict.

A critical tool in equitable planning is the special needs trust (SNT). Whether first party or third party, these trusts allow families to set aside funds for a child with disabilities while reserving their eligibility for means-tested government programs like Medicaid or Supplemental Security Income (SSI). We will discuss this tool in more detail in Chapter 10, but it is worth bringing up here because it is such an important part of the special needs estate plan.

Priya and Amar decided that a third-party SNT funded through a survivorship life insurance policy would offer them the most peace of mind. They could contribute to it throughout their lives and ensure continued funding after their deaths without risking Neel's public benefits. The trust was drafted to cover supplemental needs—transportation, recreational activities, caregiving, and other quality-of-life expenses.

By contrast, Maya and Arjun received traditional inheritances outright. This allowed Priya and Amar to simplify their estate plan while tailoring it to reflect each child's future.

Communicating the Plan

Equitable planning requires open communication, as silence often breeds misunderstanding. Priya and Amar sat down with Maya and Arjun to explain their reasoning. They talked through the costs associated with Neel's care, the need to protect his government benefits, and the emotional labor that caregiving can involve.

They reassured Maya and Arjun that their love and values were not measured by dollar signs—but that Neel's future required careful protection. The conversation wasn't easy, but it helped build a sense of shared responsibility.

The couple also included a written explanation within their estate planning documents—sometimes called a letter of intent or memorandum—to express their wishes and clarify their intentions.

This transparency reduced tension early and helped each sibling understand their role in the plan. It also provided Maya and Arjun with an opportunity to ask questions, express concerns, and clarify what future responsibilities they would be willing to accept.

Equitable Doesn't Mean Exclusive

It's important to note that equitable planning doesn't mean only one child receives an inheritance. Instead, it means recognizing that different children may need different types of support.

In some families, this could involve setting aside specific assets for a child with disabilities while offering other forms of legacy—such as education funding, property, or business interests—to siblings. Other families may create incentive trusts that encourage career or community service goals or establish family foundations where all children can participate in charitable giving.

For the Singhs, their planning involved creating three pathways: an SFT for Neel with long-term financial oversight;

529 education accounts and Roth IRAs to help Maya and Arjun build financial independence; and a shared vacation property that all siblings could enjoy and maintain jointly, strengthening their bond.

This approach allowed the Singhs to support each child while encouraging collaboration and unity.

Sibling Involvement and Expectations

Siblings play a major role in many estate plans. Whether they are named trustees, advocates, or informal caregivers, their roles should be clearly defined and thoughtfully chosen.

Involving siblings early in the planning process gives them a voice and prepares them for potential responsibilities. Priya and Amar asked Maya if she would consider serving as Neel's successor trustee—something she felt honored to do but also admitted would be challenging. To support her, they designated a professional co-trustee to handle administrative duties.

This approach helped Maya avoid burnout and allowed her to focus on being a sister, not just a fiduciary. It also provided assurance that the trust would remain compliant and professionally managed.

Parents should also consider providing other avenues of support to siblings. These might include training or introductions to legal and financial professionals, copies of letters of intent and care plans, and support networks of other families and caregivers.

These resources prepare siblings for success and reduce the risk of future family conflict.

Addressing Future Conflict

No matter how well families plan, the future can bring disagreement. That's why many estate plans include ways to address conflict. These may include mediation clauses to resolve disputes, letters of intent to document parental wishes, instructions about successor trustees and guardians, and clear policies for managing shared property or co-owned accounts.

Families should also consider how estate planning documents intersect with guardianship, powers of attorney, and healthcare proxies. Aligning these tools ensures that decision-makers are equipped to act consistently.

Priya and Amar also reviewed how Neel's care and trust would transition if Maya moved away or had children of her own. They ensured there were contingency plans in place and successor trustees named.

FINAL THOUGHTS

Estate planning isn't just about wealth—it's about values. It's about storytelling, legacy, and responsibility. In the context of a family with a member who has special needs, it's also about creating stability in the face of unpredictability.

By focusing on the unique needs of each child, families create plans that not only protect financial futures but also reinforce their most important commitments—to love, dignity, and connection.

In Priya's words: "We planned not for what we had—but for what our children needed."

Equity is not always easy. But it is always worth it.

Chapter 10

Special Needs Trusts: Their Role in Estate Planning

This chapter was written by Penelope Gaffney at Gravis Law in collaboration with the All Needs Planning team

Special needs trusts (SNTs), also called supplemental needs trusts, hold assets for a person with a disability without jeopardizing their eligibility for government benefits, such as Medicaid, Medicaid waiver programs, and Social Security. The SNTs allow the person with a disability to receive support for supplemental needs such as education, recreation, therapies, home care, transportation, and so much more. These supplemental supports are not generally covered by public benefits and can be vital to someone with a disability. Certain therapies or memberships to centers or electronic devices, as a few examples, might be vital to a disabled person's well-being, by supporting their need, community participation, and independence. As such, many families include special needs trusts in their estate planning to provide a pathway to ongoing support for their loved one.

THE TYPES OF SPECIAL NEEDS TRUSTS

SNTs are commonly arranged in one of several ways including as a first- or third-party SNT, springing or stand-alone, or as a pooled trust. (There may be variations state to state or person to person; always work with a qualified attorney to ensure your legal documents meet your needs.)

First- and Third-party SNTs

A first-party SNT, which is also sometimes called a self-settled trust, is a legal arrangement funded with the disabled person's assets in order to protect their eligibility for government benefits like Medicaid, Medicaid waiver, and Social Security. The key point is that the trust is established by the person with the disability with their assets, which is what the "first" is referring to. For example, if a disabled individual suddenly received an inheritance and the amount exceeded the Medicaid resource limit, then they could create a first-party trust to receive the funds rather than receiving them directly. In this example, the inheritance would go to the first-party SNT. Inherent in that is the requirement within first-party trusts that any remaining funds in the trust, upon the disabled person's death, may go back to the government entities to cover the cost of public benefits used.

Third-party trusts, however, are created by someone other than the disabled person, hence "third" party, and are funded with assets not owned by the person with a disability. In these cases, the SNT is funded on behalf of the person with a disability, and as such, a remainder beneficiary can usually be named so that upon the disabled member's death, any remaining funds can be directed to another person or entity. Third-party SNTs are often funded through resources established by family members and friends, such as insurance policies, retirement accounts, and properties, to name a few examples.

Springing or Stand-alone SNTs

A springing trust, which may also be called a testamentary trust or "trust under will," is a trust documented that is created while a person is alive (the person is called the grantor) but does not take effect until a specific future event occurs, such as the person's death or incapacitation. Essentially, the trust "springs" from the will and is created upon the grantor's death or incapacitation. There may be several reasons to set up an SNT this way, including not being sure if the SNT will be needed or when it is more economical for the grantor to embed the SNT in their estate planning documents.

A stand-alone SNT, on the other hand, is an SNT that is created and established separately, not within the will. By establishing the SNT as a separate entity while the grantor is alive, the SNT can be funded. The reason to do this might include wanting to have the SNT ready to receive funds, perhaps anticipating someone's death, or sometimes it helps in planning and communication with family and friends; it can help to have everything in order and established for ease of transition.

A pooled SNT is a type of legal trust management by a nonprofit organization for multiple beneficiaries with disabilities. A disabled person's pooled trust is a subaccount within a collection of other individual trusts. Pooled trusts combine the resources of many beneficiaries for purposes of administrative cost-effectiveness and to optimize investment strategy. These can also be set up as first- and third-party pooled trusts, and each state has its own rules and procedures as to what happens to the funds when the beneficiary passes. Many families choose this option as the pooled trust organizations have built-in professional supports, such as professional trustees and care managers.

A trust protector is a role within the trust document separate from the trustee. This person, professional, or entity is a neutral third party appointed in a trust document to oversee the trust and the trustee. The most important role of the trust protector is to ensure the original intent of the creator is upheld over time. In some cases, the trust protector is an attorney and is given the power to modify the trust.

A care committee is another entity within the trust designed to support your child/loved one. Similar to a microboard, it is a spelled-out group of people who support your loved one. They can be given different roles. The risk in a care committee is making sure there is a clearly defined process, they have a way to stay connected with each other, and they have a way to receive information. When done correctly, it can be a great additional support and may be less complex than coordinating a microboard.

Another important consideration in estate planning and SNTs are the regulations impacting distributions.

THE SECURE ACT

The SECURE Act refers to two pieces of legislation: SECURE Act of 2020 and SECURE Act 2.0 of 2022. These are federal laws designed to promote retirement savings and expand access to retirement plans. It includes increasing the required age for RMDs (required minimum distributions) from 72 to 73, and specifically for families of children with disabilities, it allows flexibility so that instead of requiring the beneficiary to receive the entire distribution within a 10-year period, it allows the benefit to stretch over the disabled member's lifetime. This type of legislation is an important consideration for families, particularly when deciding which assets to leave to each child. We can't stress enough how important it is to work with qualified professionals' knowledge in special needs planning when developing your estate plan and establishing your beneficiaries.

It goes without saying, there are several points to consider when determining which type of SNT makes sense for your family. The SECURE Act is one example of laws impacting your planning, but there may be others in your state or relative to your assets. It is important to also consider tax implications. Will a beneficiary face a tax consequence due to an asset they receive as an inheritance? Professional advice can help you make the most appropriate decision for your family, based on your unique situation.

The following case study illustrates important considerations in the special needs planning process.

CASE STUDY: THE MARTINEZ FAMILY

Carla and Luis Martinez are parents to three children—Sofia, Daniel, and Leo. Leo, their youngest at 11 years old, was diagnosed with a rare neurodevelopmental condition that significantly impacted his communication and mobility. Leo was full of personality—he loved music, recognized every car in the family's neighborhood, and laughed the hardest at his sister's jokes. But his needs were intensive, and Carla and Luis often found themselves juggling their full-time jobs, raising their other children, and ensuring Leo's needs are met.

They had established a will years ago, but as Leo's needs became clearer, they started to ask more urgent questions. What happens to Leo if something happens to us? Will our other children have the resources—and desire—to care for Leo? What is the best way to protect Leo without putting all responsibility on his siblings? These questions led them to explore comprehensive estate planning for their entire family.

Building Blocks of a Thoughtful Plan

The Martinez family worked with a knowledgeable estate planning attorney who guided them through the tools and strategies that best fit Leo's needs. First, they focused on identifying the right type of trust for Leo's situation. In their case, a third-party stand-alone special needs trust was the ideal choice. This type of trust would not count against Leo's eligibility for government programs like Medicaid and SSI, and it would allow his parents and other relatives to contribute without triggering penalties.

Unlike a testamentary trust, which comes into effect only after the death of the settlor, a stand-alone trust can be used during the lifetime of the parent and offers greater flexibility. Leo's trust could be funded gradually over time, through gifts, inheritances, and life insurance proceeds. More importantly, it could be structured to last for Leo's lifetime and beyond.

Planning for continuity also means anticipating changes in laws, benefits, and Leo's abilities. The attorney helped the family understand how to structure distributions so they wouldn't inadvertently disqualify Leo from means-tested programs. Expenses for basic living needs—such as housing or food—were excluded, while therapies, technology, recreation, and supplemental education were covered.

To ensure proper oversight, Carla and Luis appointed a trustee who not only had financial management experience but also a deep understanding of Leo's needs. They added a trust protector to monitor the trustee's actions and step in if the trustee failed in their responsibilities. They also formed a microboard—a team of family, educators, and service providers—who could offer input and feedback about Leo's well-being and evolving needs.

Trust protectors and care committees both serve as safeguards—added protection and barriers to error—to maintain Leo's well-being. Trust protectors promote accountability, ensuring the trustee is acting in Leo's best interests. A care committee offers a personalized check-in system to adjust plans and support Leo even as he grows. Together, they create a collaborative framework for managing the trust and assuring that Leo is always taken care of.

Anticipating Transition Points

A critical part of the plan was anticipating Leo's transition into adulthood. At age 18, Leo would become a legal adult, even if he was not able to make independent decisions. Carla and Luis considered various decision-making support tools, including guardianship, supported decision-making, and durable power of attorney. They were also able to supplement with their existing microboard. Guardianship might be necessary if Leo could not communicate his preferences. However, they were also open to using supported decision-making paired with a power of attorney to the extent that Leo could participate in the process.

The decision-making landscape for adults with disabilities is complex. Guardianship, while protective, can also limit autonomy. Supported decision-making, a less restrictive alternative, enables the individual to make decisions with help from trusted advisors. The Martinez family worked with advocates and attorneys to evaluate these options based on Leo's capacity, preferences, and likely future needs.

Medical directives and living wills were also addressed, in case Leo's health deteriorated or if emergency decisions needed to be made. The estate plan outlined preferred providers, care philosophies, and directions for long-term care funding. This gave both Carla and Luis peace of mind that their wishes would be honored and that Leo's needs would not be left to guesswork.

In the end, they worked with Leo and their attorney to coordinate a power of attorney with a microboard to give Leo the decision-making support he needed. There is much more information on supported decision-making in Chapter 11.

Housing was another major consideration. Carla and Luis hoped to keep Leo at home as long as possible, but they also began exploring supported housing models for the future. They researched group homes, host home arrangements, and shared living environments that could provide stability, companionship, and professional oversight.

Planning for Minor Children and Siblings

Estate planning is not just about the child with disabilities—it's about the entire family. Carla and Luis did not want Sofia and Daniel to feel burdened or overlooked. They engaged in conversations with both children, explaining the planning process and the reasons for certain financial allocations. They emphasized fairness over equality.

Siblings often carry invisible emotional and logistical weight. They may feel pressure to step into caregiving roles, resolve disputes, or advocate for their sibling without preparation or support. The Martinez family addressed these dynamics directly, inviting Sofia and Daniel into the planning conversations and making sure their voices were heard.

Sofia and Daniel were designated as potential future guardians for Leo, but only with their full agreement. Carla and Luis also considered how Leo's needs might shift over time and left flexibility in the plan to adjust roles and responsibilities. Recognizing that circumstances can change—such as health issues or changes in personal capacity—the couple named backup guardians and trustees in case the primary appointees were unable or unwilling to serve. Having backups was important to Carla and Luis to ensure that Leo would remain stably supported even if one of the existing guardians had to back out—it gave them peace of mind that Leo would always be cared for by someone who knows and loves him, even if life took an unexpected turn.

Carla and Luis purchased a life insurance policy specifically to fund Leo's trust. This strategy ensured that their other assets could be passed to Sofia and Daniel without diminishing Leo's resources. They also wrote letters of intent—personal documents explaining their values, Leo's preferences, and their hopes for the future. These letters were not legally binding, but they provided context and humanity that no legal document could capture.

Legal Considerations

The Martinez family's attorney referenced multiple legal precedents to guide the plan. *Hobbs ex rel. Hobbs v. Zenderman* underscored the importance of meeting

Medicaid trust exemption requirements. *Ramey v. Rizzuto* and *National Foundation for Special Needs Integrity v. Reese* highlighted the distinction between first-party and third-party trusts and the treatment of residual assets. The care committee structure and role of trust protectors were modeled after best practices from *Cobell v. Norton*. Together, these cases built a strong legal foundation for the Martinez plan.

Equitable planning requires precise language in the trust documents to avoid benefit disruption. The attorney carefully structured the distributions to be discretionary and non-mandatory, ensuring compliance with public benefit rules. The trust prohibited payments for basic needs covered by SSI but allowed enhancements such as educational experiences, therapy, and recreation.

Federal regulations also influenced the decision-making framework. The family reviewed options under 42 U.S.C. §§ 405 and 1383 concerning misuse of Social Security benefits and representative payees. They documented Leo's eligibility, evaluated potential misuse of safeguards, and consulted professionals about tracking and auditing.

The Emotional Impact

Throughout the process, Carla and Luis were struck by how emotional estate planning could be. Each decision felt weighty—shaped by love, fear, responsibility, and hope. They had to confront their own mortality, their son's lifelong vulnerability, and the unpredictability of the future.

They also found support in their community by connecting with other families facing similar choices. Support groups, advocacy organizations, and legal clinics became sounding boards and sources of comfort. Hearing other parents' experiences validated their concerns and gave them ideas they hadn't considered.

But by the end of the process, they experienced clarity and empowerment. They knew who would step in, what resources would be available, and how their family would be protected. Estate planning transformed from a task to a gift—a tangible expression of their love for Leo and their trust in Sofia and Daniel.

The process also brought the couple closer. Talking about hopes, fears, and dreams for their children deepened their communication. They laughed, cried, and collaborated more meaningfully than they had in years. They discovered that estate planning wasn't just about logistics—it was about legacy.

Estate planning for a special needs family is both a legal responsibility and a heartfelt journey. The process requires thoughtful customization, collaboration with professionals, and open family dialogue. With the right guidance, families can create plans that safeguard benefits, respect individual dignity, and honor the family's shared values.

For the Martinez family, planning wasn't about control—it was about care. It wasn't about predicting the future—it was about preparing for it, together.

KEY LEGAL PRECEDENTS AND QUESTIONS FOR CONSIDERATION

As families work with estate planning professionals to design or update their special needs estate plans, it is essential to consider the legal precedents that shape these tools.

The following cases provide a framework for interpreting how trusts, benefits, and fiduciary roles must be structured and administered:

- *Hobbs ex rel. Hobbs v. Zenderman*, 579 F.3d 1171 (10th Cir. 2009)
- *Ramey v. Rizzuto*, 72 F. Supp. 2d 1202 (D. Colo. 1999)
- *National Foundation for Special Needs Integrity, Inc. v. Reese*, 881 F.3d 1023 (10th Cir. 2018)
- *Cobell v. Norton*, 240 F.3d 1081 (D.C. Cir. 2001)
- *Lewis v. Alexander*, 685 F.3d 325 (3d Cir. 2012)

These cases collectively underscore the principles of compliance, beneficiary protection, state recovery obligations, and fiduciary accountability. To guide families and practitioners through the planning process, the following questions can serve as a helpful starting point:

- Does your trust document clearly identify whether it is a first-party or third-party special needs trust, and does it meet the specific requirements outlined in *Hobbs v. Zenderman* for exemption from Medicaid spend-down calculations?
- Have you reviewed and accounted for the role of discretionary distributions in your trust language, ensuring compliance with *Ramey v. Rizzuto*?
- If residual funds exist after the beneficiary's death, have you specified successor beneficiaries in a way that reflects the allowance recognized in *Reese*?
- Have you considered appointing a trust protector or a care committee to oversee the trustee, as recommended in *Cobell v. Norton*?
- If your loved one may benefit from a pooled trust, have you compared the administrative structures addressed in *Lewis v. Alexander* and evaluated nonprofit management options?

These legal decisions are not just academic—they impact how trusts are interpreted, how benefits are preserved, and how families can best plan for lifelong care. Incorporating these principles into your estate planning documents ensures that the plan is robust, defensible, and aligned with public benefit eligibility rules.

FINAL THOUGHTS

The process of estate planning for a loved one with special needs is not a one-time event—it is a living, breathing expression of care that must evolve with time, changing laws, and the dynamic needs of the individual. Families who take on this journey, like the Martinez family, are not only engaging in responsible planning—they are laying the groundwork for intergenerational resilience, compassion, and dignity.

Throughout this chapter, we have examined the layers that comprise an effective plan: legal compliance, thoughtful trustee and guardian selection, equitable financial distribution, and mechanisms for oversight and adaptability. These elements are vital, but perhaps the most transformative piece is the shift in mindset. Estate planning is not simply about fear of the unknown—it's about hope for the future. It is an opportunity to affirm the inherent worth of every family member and provide a blueprint for their care, their autonomy, and their legacy.

When families complete their plans, what they often feel is not just relief but empowerment. They've turned a sense of powerlessness into a proactive commitment. They've navigated emotional terrain and emerged with clarity, purpose, and protection for the ones they love. This clarity ripples outward, empowering siblings, extended family, educators, and professionals who support individuals with special needs.

Ultimately, the tools we've discussed—trusts, directives, and guardianships—are instruments. But the music comes from the intention behind them. That intention must be loving, informed, inclusive, and, most importantly, continuous. Plans should be revisited regularly, discussed openly, and amended as needs evolve. They are not monuments but maps—tools that guide, not define.

As you take the next step in your own estate planning journey, remember this: no family is too small, too busy, or too uncertain to begin. Starting is the most important step. With support from knowledgeable legal counsel, financial advisors, and your broader community, your family can build a plan that sustains both care and peace of mind.

In closing, Carla and Luis remind us that while the process may seem overwhelming at first, its impact is lasting: "It's not just about making sure Leo is okay when we're gone. It's about making sure he thrives while we're still here—and long after."

Estate planning for your special needs family is a powerful act of love. May this chapter be your invitation to begin.

Chapter 11

Decision-making Support: Balancing Protection and Autonomy

Across the country—and the globe—there is increasing recognition that individuals with disabilities have the same human rights as everyone else, including the right to make choices about their own lives. This has sparked a growing movement toward supported decision-making as a preferred model of care, which encourages collaboration without legally removing someone's rights. In 2006, the United Nations adopted the Convention on the Rights of Persons with Disabilities (CRPD), urging countries to respect the autonomy, dignity, and legal capacity of individuals with disabilities. While the United States has signed the CRPD, its principles are only slowly making their way into legal frameworks.[1]

Critics of guardianship systems argue that full guardianship removes an individual's civil rights—such as voting, deciding where to live, or getting married—often with no opportunity for restoration, and therefore supported decision-making (SDM) has become the rallying cry for disability rights advocates pushing for systems that uphold dignity and autonomy.[2,3]

But in practice, families are often left with difficult decisions. Autonomy must be weighed against the very real threat of exploitation, abuse, or neglect. We've worked with countless families who want to honor their loved one's independence but also recognize that their child is vulnerable to being manipulated by others or simply overwhelmed by complex systems.

Our perspective is that we believe in protecting autonomy whenever possible, but we also understand that safety, dignity, and support are core components of a meaningful life. We strive to meet families where they are, helping them evaluate the full spectrum of decision-making supports—from the least restrictive to more formal options like guardianship—based on their loved one's actual needs. We'll explore the continuum of support options in this chapter, from supported decision-making to powers of attorney to guardianship. We'll also look at how microboards can play a stabilizing role across all these structures.

But first let's begin with Toni's story.

CASE STUDY: TONI'S STORY

Toni is turning 18 soon, and his moms—Sarah and Lisa—are thinking through how to support him as he becomes a legal adult. Toni is thoughtful, bright, and independent in many areas. He's finishing high school with a standard diploma and works part-time at a local grocery store. His dream is to pursue coding classes at the community college and increase his work hours.

Still, his moms are concerned. Toni, who has 22q11.2 deletion syndrome, can be socially vulnerable. He might have trouble identifying when someone is taking advantage of him. He relies on reminders for certain responsibilities and needs support navigating medical and financial systems.

The family sits down to talk. They want Toni to maintain as much independence as possible, but they also know that when he turns 18, they won't automatically have access to his medical or educational information—or the ability to advocate on his behalf. They discuss having Toni appoint them as his agents under a power of attorney and advance medical directive. They also begin organizing a microboard: a small group of trusted adults who can serve as long-term supporters and advocates, which we'll cover later in this chapter.

This thoughtful approach—balancing autonomy with proactive planning—is a powerful example of what decision-making support can look like in real life.

THE CONTINUUM OF SUPPORT

Decision-making support exists on a spectrum, ranging from informal collaboration to full legal guardianship. The following text breaks down the most common tools, from least restrictive to most.

Supported Decision-making

SDM allows individuals with disabilities to choose supporters who help them understand, consider, and communicate decisions—without transferring any legal rights. This model promotes autonomy and dignity and is increasingly recognized in some US states through formal agreements.[4]

The benefits of SDM are many. SDM preserves all legal rights of the individual and ensures that the person with the disability is making decisions for their own behalf. It allows them to make mistakes and to own those mistakes. A great example is a person with intellectual disability who chooses to have donuts for breakfast every day. We all know that donuts for breakfast aren't healthy. But almost all humans are able to choose what they have for breakfast.

Supported decision-making goes broader than what you have for breakfast. It allows a person with a disability to seek support when needed, take that support into consideration, and then make the best decision for themselves. It also allows them to still vote, and encourages personal agency, responsibility, and independence.

But there are limitations as well. Supported decision-making is not legally binding in most states. And because supported decision-making documents say that the person who is being supported still needs to make the final decision, it does not allow someone else to make decisions on their behalf. It may not be recognized by healthcare or financial institutions, not just in terms of decision-making support but also in allowing access to records and to be a part of medical conversations.

If these are areas that your loved one needs support, you might consider using SDM as well as power of attorney and medical directive.

You will also want to consider that SDM requires the person with a disability to be proactive in seeking support and does not have a mechanism for replacing someone who is no longer able to serve in a supportive role to the person. That means that the disabled individual must be able to think through multistep thoughts and reach out. They will also need to remember who their supportive decision-makers are and when the proper time to reach out is. Depending on their level and type of disability, this may or may not be appropriate for them.

Power of Attorney and Medical Directive

If a person is deemed competent, they can voluntarily sign a power of attorney (POA), naming someone they trust to help manage financial or healthcare decisions. A medical directive (or advance directive) lays out preferences for care if the individual becomes incapacitated.

If an individual cannot understand and consent to a POA, an attorney may refuse to draft one. In these cases, a more formal legal arrangement—like guardianship—may be necessary.

We want to point out that POA documents do not allow a POA to override the wishes of an individual. For example, if the individual is over 18 and expressly states that they do not want to engage in a certain treatment for their illness, a medical POA cannot legally override them and force them to be treated. We have found that many people are unaware of this nuance.

POA also does not allow someone to do things that are directly against the person's self-interest. A POA could not alter someone's will to make themselves the beneficiary, for example, or add themselves to the person's bank account without their permission, draining funds for their own benefit.

We also recognize that there is "what's legal" and then there is the fraud and abuse that actually happens. We strongly encourage that there be multiple levels of safeguards in place for all individuals to protect against fraud and abuse. A microboard is a great tool for this that we will cover in more depth later in the chapter.

We recommend that every individual have a POA and medical directive in place with a trusted family member or friend who can serve on their behalf. While some have lifelong disabilities, almost every human has a time where they are incapacitated and need help in making decisions, managing financial accounts, and more. Whether it is from a car accident, getting older, or a workplace injury, there are many different ways we become disabled. A POA and medical directive will allow for that decision-making support to be available when needed.

> **NOTE:** When someone receives SSI or SSDI but cannot manage the funds themselves, the Social Security Administration can appoint a Representative Payee to manage the money. This process is separate from guardianship and does not require a court proceeding.[5]

Guardianship and Conservatorship

If a person lacks the capacity to make decisions, a court may appoint a guardian (for personal and medical decisions) and/or conservator (for financial matters). Some states use both terms; others combine the roles.

The court process for guardianship and/or conservatorship has several basic parts: filing a petition, evaluating capacity, holding a court hearing to review the petition and evaluation as well as to review any potential or nominated guardian, and finalizing the guardianship. In that first step, the petition provides information about the individual, the proposed guardian, and relevant background information such as psychological evaluations, medical information, and any other documentation that speaks to the capacity of the individual.

The court uses this information when evaluating the petition and in determining guardianship. Your local court system will have information and required documentation for this process and there are usually local attorneys who specialize in guardianship.

There are key considerations for guardianship. Guardianship can be limited. An individual might retain certain rights (e.g., voting or driving) while a guardian handles others. Families should revisit and revise guardianships over time to reflect changing abilities. In some cases, a person under guardianship may even retain the right to own a firearm, though this varies widely by state.[6]

Case Study: The Very Public Conservatorship of Britney Spears

In 2008, Britney Spears was hospitalized under a 72-hour psychiatric hold after refusing to relinquish custody of her children to ex-husband Kevin Federline. Shortly after that a California court approved a temporary conservatorship with Jamie Spears, her father, as co-conservator, due to concerns about her inability to make her own personal and financial decisions. The temporary conservatorship was changed to permanent shortly after and lasted until 2021 after Britney fought to end it. Her battle to end her conservatorship was of tremendous public interest as it brought to light concerns many have about the processes involved in guardianship and conservatorship. The Free Britney Act of California, which was signed into law in 2021, put more processes in place to guide the court's ruling and to protect individuals for whom others are seeking guardianship or conservatorship.

It is our firm belief that no guardian should be able to sign a contract that compels the individual under guardianship to fulfill certain obligations: working, performing, etc. That crosses an ethical line and should never be allowed. It also allows an inherent conflict of interest to come into play, especially in a case such as Britney where her father was acting as her manager and making significant profit on her working.

RISK OF INACTION

Without any formal supports in place, a young adult turning 18 could face serious difficulties. Their parents may be unable to access medical information or make appointments, assist with financial decisions, and advocate during emergencies.

Additionally, families may not be invited to IEP meetings or be involved in/communicated with about school decisions. Since many disabled individuals stay in school through age 21–22, this can provide a real obstruction in supporting the individual.

We've worked with families where these gaps led to medical crises, disrupted services, or even exploitation. One distraught mother let us know that her son had been hospitalized for months as a result of not eating, had dropped out of college (that she had been continuing to pay for), and she hadn't heard from him. She had called every hospital in the area, and none would release any information to her. Her son had selective mutism and had stopped communicating the second he was hospitalized. It was six months later that she finally heard from him that he was okay.

Planning ahead can prevent costly and distressing outcomes.

HOW MICROBOARDS FIT IN

Microboards are small organizations created by and for an individual with a disability. They are formal circles of support—with bylaws, a board of directors, officers, and a running agenda—that are often organized as a nonprofit or nonstock corporation (depending on the state).

They serve as an advocacy team—friends, family, community members, and professionals—who work together to support the person's goals and well-being. Microboards can provide continuity, oversight, and guidance no matter what legal tools are in place.

Whether the individual uses SDM, POA, or guardianship, the microboard can serve as a built-in network of eyes and ears. They can attend planning meetings, ensure the person's values and preferences are honored, and help navigate transitions or emergencies. Importantly, a microboard is a formal entity. There is a running agenda, with bylaws that include the wishes of those who established the microboard. They are designed to be person-centered in supporting the individual. There are requirements to have annual meeting minutes. They can meet at a minimum of once a year, or as often as they feel is necessary—for example, they may meet more often during a crisis period.

We have found that most (or many) people are familiar with the experience of being on a formal board. After serving for some time, a magical thing happens. Board members of the microboard start to think proactively in supporting the individual. No longer are the parents running everything. We have watched microboards help support parents to take vacations away from their children. Come in proactively to support a parent going through a health crisis. And guide a trustee in how to find the right professionals to continue supporting their loved one.

Microboards can also serve as a critical part of long-term planning—especially as parents age or pass away. They can also be written into a family's estate plan to provide support to the trustee and/or executor to aid in how assets are distributed. A microboard may, for example, help a trustee decide where the disabled individual should live after a parent passes away. Perhaps the intent was for them to live in the family home, but supports are not available for that to be a successful outcome. They can help guide the trustee, the guardian, and the disabled individual to make a successful transition during an extremely stressful time.

Another great part of having a microboard is that you can include caring family members, friends, and supporters who may have offered to provide support but don't know how. Perhaps they live far away and have not been involved in your day-to-day lives. Being on a microboard is not a huge time commitment. It's a low-commitment/high-value activity—and we find that many family members who were overwhelmed with the idea of providing daily supports are much more open to providing support by serving on a microboard.

Microboards can also be an important sibling support. Often siblings are designated as trustee, guardian, and expected to have their sibling with a disability live with them. Some siblings are fine with this—we often see siblings devote their lives to supporting a sibling with a disability—but siblings' lives often change and become more complex. They may be supporting their own family, have troubles of their own, or have children of their own with disabilities that they are struggling to navigate supports with. A microboard can extend their support system and make sure they can access the services and supports needed for their sibling—and themselves.

We often call the microboard the magic bullet of special needs planning. The proof is in the pudding: you get a proactive team helping you and your family, with a formal process to follow. And don't forget—a microboard can exist as a stand-alone type of decision-making support, but we recommend you use it alongside a POA/medical directive or guardianship. It's not an either/or—it's yes/and.

SUMMARY OF SUPPORT METHODS

Table 11.1 summarizes the support methods we've discussed in this chapter. This table can serve as a starting point to figure out what types of decision-making support your loved one needs.

Decision-making support is not one-size-fits-all. It's a framework built around the individual's needs, abilities, and values. By understanding the tools available—and combining them with real-life supports like microboards—families can protect autonomy while safeguarding their loved one's future.

CASE STUDY: WHEN SUPPORT TURNS INTO CONTROL

Carlos is a 28-year-old man with mild intellectual disability. He lives in a licensed group home that provides supervision and personal care. Carlos has expressed that he likes staying up late on weekends and occasionally wants a snack before bed. One Friday night, he was hungry at 11:00 p.m. and saw leftover pizza in the refrigerator.

When Carlos asked staff if he could have a slice, he was told, "the kitchen is closed." This wasn't about dietary restrictions—he simply wasn't permitted to eat on his own

Table 11.1 Support Methods

Support Method	Best Used When	Key Features
Supported decision-making (SDM)	Individual can make decisions with guidance and wants to retain all rights.	Preserves all legal rights; not legally binding in all states
Power of attorney (POA)	Individual is competent and wants to designate someone to help with finances or decisions.	Voluntary legal agreement; ends if the person becomes incapacitated or revokes it
Medical directive/living will	Individual is competent and wants to document medical preferences in advance.	Specifies care wishes if individual cannot express them later
Representative payee	Individual receives Social Security benefits but cannot manage money independently.	Appointed by SSA; manages benefits only
Guardianship/ conservatorship	Individual lacks decision-making capacity and needs formal legal support.	Court-appointed; can be limited or full; restricts legal rights
Microboard	Family wants a long-term support network to guide advocacy and oversight across the lifespan.	Nonprofit board of advocates; complements any legal support structure

schedule. The decision had nothing to do with his health or behavior. He wasn't trusted to access his own food.

While group homes are often staffed by well-meaning people, policies may default to control rather than empowerment. Denying an adult the ability to eat food that is already in the house—especially food that may have been bought for them—can be a violation of their human rights. Autonomy must not be overridden for convenience.

Legal advocacy organizations have pointed out that unnecessarily restrictive policies can violate federal disability rights laws, including the Americans with Disabilities Act (ADA) and the *Olmstead v. L.C.* Supreme Court decision, which mandates that individuals with disabilities receive services in the most integrated setting appropriate to their needs.

Autonomy and decision-making go hand in hand. However, it is important to recognize that although an individual may need support in their decision-making, that does not mean they should lose all of their autonomy. Finding ways to support their ability to make their own decisions and have control over their daily lives is important to preserve their dignity and enhance their quality of life.

FINAL THOUGHTS

There is help in decision-making. Attorneys, advocates, doctors, and other trusted professionals can help you and your loved one talk through the options. Be sure to take advantage of the resources around you to provide guidance and support during this process.

Chapter 12

Investing for Two Lifetimes: Building Enduring Wealth Through Income and Growth

Thousands of investment professionals are focused on investing. From financial advisors to chief investment officers, there are just as many different opinions about how to invest as there are professionals.

As you approach this process, the important thing to remember is that you are investing for two lifetimes. You are not putting a pot of money away and then using it 50 years later. You will need to use it for your own retirement (and your spouse, if applicable), and then also for the life of your child.

Of course, performance is important. I would suggest that even more important is understanding the risks that are inherent to investing over this period. You do not want to invest like an institution because you need to have access to the money. Institutions often obtain superior returns by investing in riskier assets as well as assets that are not liquid or require decades to see the returns.

When you look at the assets your family has, you want to understand what the returns of each asset are—and the risks that are inherent to each of those returns. Go back to the earlier chapter where we looked at financial planning and identified income streams. Will your income streams provide enough income for your family in retirement? Tally up your Social Security, pension, real estate income, and compare that to your budget.

For most families, the income streams are not enough. You need to supplement that from your investments. This chapter will focus on those investments—and how you can be more efficient with your investments, potentially reduce risk, and use the same investments for your retirement as you use to support your loved one throughout their lifetime.

We believe income investing—and specifically, dividend income investing—is the key.

CASE STUDY: MELINDA AND KATIE

Melinda is a 58-year-old professional and a single parent to 11-year-old Katie, who has a rare genetic disorder. Katie is thriving in school with the help of a strong IEP team, and Melinda has done a great job advocating for her daughter's needs. As Melinda looks ahead, she wonders how and when she will be able to retire—and, more importantly, how to ensure Katie has the resources she will need for the rest of her life.

Melinda knows she may not be here for Katie's entire life. That means her investments need to do more than support her own retirement—they need to last through Katie's adulthood too. In other words, she needs a strategy that works across two lifetimes.

Melinda made the assumption that many special needs parents make—she assumed that she was going to have to work forever. While she made good money, she did not believe it would be enough for Katie. At 11, Katie had an IEP but not a Medicaid waiver. Her genetic disorder is degenerative, and she will need more support as she ages. Melinda is plugged in as much as she can, but she always feels she will need more money. Her biggest fear is Melinda running out of money.

With careful investment management and planning, Melinda was able to see that her hard work could be put into a strategy that would provide for her own retirement as well as Katie's lifetime. Read on to learn more about the investment strategy that brought Melinda peace of mind.

INVESTING FOR INCOME: WHY DIVIDENDS MATTER

When planning for a longer horizon, particularly in the context of special needs planning, dividend investing offers one of the most powerful solutions available. A dividend-focused strategy not only generates income—it helps preserve capital and reduces emotional decision-making during market volatility.

First let's cover the basics with some definitions. A stock is a share (or percentage) of ownership in a company. So, if you own a stock, you own shares of a company. A company's leadership always has two choices: to reinvest their profits (after covering expenses) to focus on future growth or to pay the profits out to the owners (stockholders or shareholders) in the form of a dividend. Dividend-paying stocks are also called value stocks. So, you may hear, as you are listening to investment strategists, people talking about growth versus value stocks—that's what they mean!

Now how do you know if you are buying a stock that pays a dividend? Quite simply, you look it up. Start familiarizing yourself with financial sites such as Morningstar.com where you can look up if a company pays a dividend.

A bond, on the other hand, is someone loaning a company money in exchange for interest. The terms of the bond control how long the loan is for, what the interest rate is, and how often it is paid. If you own bonds, you are the lender—and the company is the borrower.

Now let's give you a couple of other quick definitions. As a smaller investor (meaning, you are not an institution with billions of dollars to invest), you may want more diversification than buying individual stocks would allow you. In that case, you can buy a basket of securities through mutual funds or exchange traded funds.

A mutual fund is a basket of securities that is typically managed by a portfolio manager, who is choosing the individual securities inside. Mutual funds have a lot of advantages—we do want to point out there are some disadvantages to owning mutual funds in taxable accounts. You don't always know exactly what stocks and bonds you are buying in mutual funds—managers are not required to be transparent with their holdings. You may also experience something called phantom capital gains—where someone else sells out of the fund and the manager must sell out of securities. If those securities have taxable gains, those taxable gains are passed onto the current shareholders—not the ones who sold them. When this happens, you could end up paying taxes, even when the fund has declined in value. No one likes paying taxes when they have actually lost money!

Exchange traded funds are a more modern investment instrument that have eliminated the so-called phantom capital gains. Please do not take this to mean that you do not owe taxes on exchange traded funds—you do still pay taxes; the good news is that you are paying taxes on your own capital gains (the price you purchased the ETF at versus the price you sold), dividends, and interest accrued in the fund. Exchange traded funds are usually—but not always—passive investments, meaning that there is an index of securities that are put together by rules or a committee who chooses the investment and their weights. There is no individual manager who is choosing when to buy or sell.

Both exchange traded funds and mutual funds have underlying costs that a buyer/owner must pay. These costs are expenses charged to the owner of the fund to cover the cost of investing, pay the portfolio manager, and others involved in managing the fund. Paying attention to your overall costs is a really important part of planning over multiple generations. We will talk more about cost later in this chapter.

We believe that all investments may have a place in a portfolio. But what we have seen as the most powerful tool in multigenerational planning for special needs families are dividend-paying stocks. Working with a financial advisor who invests in individual dividend-paying stocks is also a great way to eliminate the cost of paying for an additional manager. You will hear this throughout this chapter—investing is not only about making money. It's also about controlling costs. As John Bogle wrote (the founder of the Vanguard Group), "low costs enable lower risk portfolios to provide higher returns than higher risk portfolios."

As economist Jeremy Siegel notes in *Stocks for the Long Run* and *The Future for Investors*, dividend-paying stocks have historically outperformed growth stocks over long time horizons. Reinvested dividends account for a significant share of the total return in the stock market.[1]

When you are in asset accumulation stage, we do recommend that you balance dividend investing with growth stocks. Technology stocks have provided for much of the growth of the S&P 500 in recent years. But as you get closer to retirement, increasing your dividend-paying stocks to be a larger portion of your portfolio just makes sense.

This is why dividends work for two lifetimes. Dividends provide consistent income. A stream of income can help support your retirement—and later, your loved one's care—even when the market is volatile. They also reduce reliance on selling shares. Selling principal in a down market can derail long-term plans. Income from dividends helps avoid that. Dividends also encourage long-term thinking. A dividend-paying portfolio tends to include companies with stable, resilient business models.

And here is one of the biggest reasons I like dividends today (and every day): they offer a moment of truth in an uncertain world. In markets that seem driven by speculation, inflated valuations, and headline risk, dividends offer something refreshingly real. Companies can manipulate earnings or forecast rosy projections, but dividends are either paid—or they're not. That clarity creates a foundation of stability. Over time, consistent dividend payments indicate a business with a strong balance sheet and disciplined leadership.

Dividends also represent choice and freedom. When the company pays you, it acknowledges that you—as the investor—may have better use for those funds than the company does for reinvestment. And what we know, friends, is that your family has a better use for those funds than the company does: supporting your family's retirement and your loved one's cost of care.

GROWTH VERSUS DIVIDEND INVESTING

We're often asked why we emphasize dividend investing over growth investing. The answer lies in the goals of our families.

Growth investing—especially in sectors like technology—can provide impressive returns, but it typically comes with more volatility and fewer income distributions. While younger families may benefit from some exposure to growth-oriented sectors (because they often fuel innovation and future wealth), a strategy heavily tilted toward growth can pose challenges when you start drawing on the portfolio.

We include growth in our portfolios—but we use it in small amounts and pair it with strong dividend strategies to ensure the portfolio can do both: achieve growth through the compounded returns of reinvesting dividends (keep reading to learn more about the magic of compounding), get exposure to high-growth technology stocks that are higher risk and also provide generally higher returns, then shift to generate income on your portfolio for you to live on when you're older.

SEQUENCE OF RETURNS RISK

One of the greatest risks in retirement planning is sequence of returns risk—the danger that poor market returns in early retirement force you to sell assets at a loss. This can significantly shorten how long a portfolio lasts.

Let's say you retire into a bear market. If your way to meet your family's income needs is to sell existing assets/investments, those losses become permanent. This puts much more pressure on the rest of your portfolio to make up for the loss or risk running out of money.

A dividend strategy helps mitigate this by creating a natural income stream without needing to sell shares. And when the market comes back, the value of the shares will likely come back too—meaning that you stayed with what we would call a "paper loss"—meaning you saw a loss on your statements, but since you never sold the stocks, you didn't realize the loss. You may be asking—why purchase dividend-paying stocks rather than purchasing bonds? Bonds are lower risk since you are lending the company money rather than becoming an owner of the company, so this might seem to be the best option at first glance. However, there is one very important distinction: a dividend-paying stock has the opportunity to not only pay you a dividend, but also for the price to appreciate. A bond issued at par value will redeem at par value. In long-term investing—especially for money meant to last over two generations—stocks have been the key (and we believe will continue to be the key) to maintaining and growing wealth. Bonds are an important diversifier and can control the risk of a portfolio, but they should not be the majority of the portfolio for most investors.

Dividend income acts as a buffer—helping you weather down years without touching your principal. And investing in dividend-paying stocks allows you to not only receive dividends, but to give you the potential of capital appreciation as well.

RISK OF EMOTIONAL INVESTING

Sequence of returns risk is not the only risk to worry about with investing. One of the other key risks that families face—that can be even more challenging for special needs families—is how to stay invested during tumultuous times.

A prudent investor buys investments at the lowest price and sells at the highest price. Now of course if we were able to time the market perfectly, we would all be billionaires. But most of us—when left to our own devices—have a tendency to buy at the top and sell at the bottom.

Think about it. Warren Buffett famously said, "Buy when there's blood in the streets." What he meant is that when everything looks darkest—when every single person you hear on TV is talking negatively about the markets, the economy is in a downward spiral, and your neighbors are talking at parties about how much money they've lost in the stock market—that is the best time to buy. But it will not feel like the best time to buy. It will feel like the worst time to buy. No one you know will be buying. But truly, that is the best time to put your money to work.

The reason most of us do not do that is that our emotions get in the way. For families with a special needs child, this can be especially true. Your emotions are telling you all kinds of stories. That this time is the time the market will never come back. The world is scarier now. It will feel like there are a million reasons to sell at a loss and get back to a "safe place"—where you are not taking risk.

For most people who do this—and every financial advisor has tried to counsel a client to not do this, only to watch them lock in a loss—they never recover from the loss. They miss the market recovery (market recoveries happen fast and with little notice—there is a lot of research showing if you miss the top performing days in the market, you lose most of the performance of the market) and therefore their portfolios don't prepare them for their future goals.

One of the best ways to avoid emotional investing is to work with a financial planner. Put together a plan and an investment strategy. Talk through with them what a market downturn might look like and feel like. Commit to staying the course.

And if you are feeling a bit like Warren Buffet, you might even commit to putting some cash you have in the stock market when you are feeling the worst.

THE POWER OF REINVESTMENT AND DOLLAR COST AVERAGING

Dividend reinvestment is not just a "set it and forget it" tactic—it's a disciplined way to build wealth. Each time a dividend is paid and reinvested, you're buying more shares—often at varying prices. This is essentially *dollar cost averaging* in action.

Dollar cost averaging spreads out the purchase of shares over time. It smooths the entry points into the market and helps reduce the risk of investing a large amount right before a market drop.

When dividends are reinvested, investors purchase more shares when prices are lower and fewer shares when prices are higher, creating a natural discipline that benefits long-term wealth accumulation. Figure 12.1 shows the impact of dividend reinvestment over time, and Figure 12.2 shows the contribution of dividends to total return. What you'll see from both figures is that there is also a compounding effect of reinvesting your dividends—in other words, the more shares you are buying from reinvesting dividends, the more dividends you are receiving in the future, and the more value/money you have in the long run. You can see this in evidence in Figure 12.1 where the yellow line skews higher up on the right than the orange line—the difference between the two lines becomes larger over time.

As a leading dividend investor, David Scranton from Sound Income Strategies often says to think of investing like riding

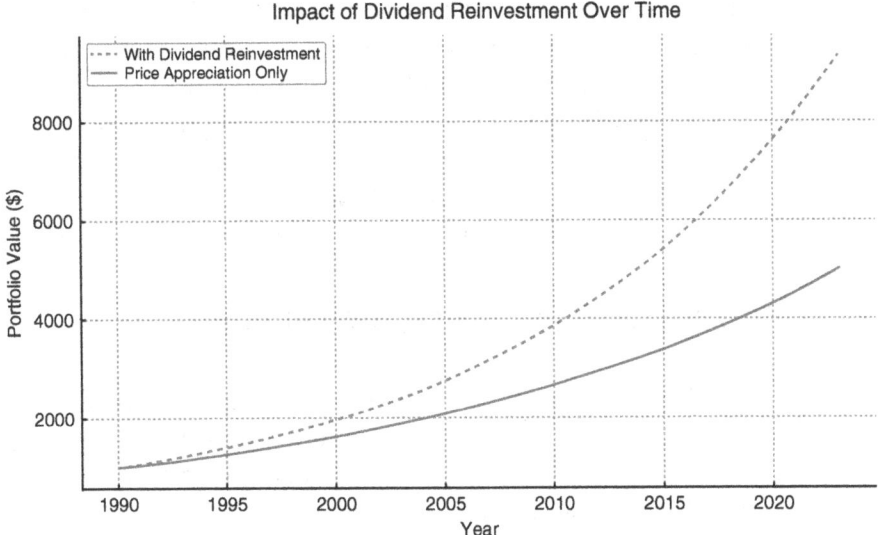

Figure 12.1 Impact of dividend reinvestment over time.
Source: Adapted from Hartford Funds, 2024.

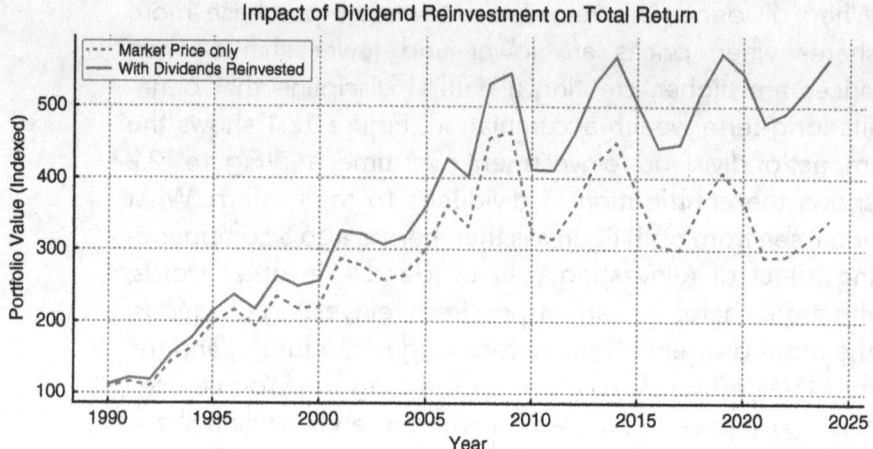

Figure 12.2 **Contribution of dividends to total return (1926–2023).**
Source: Adapted from Hartford Funds, 2024.

a bike. If you watch professional riders in the peloton, they often ride one behind the other in a position called drafting. The draft allows the rider behind to achieve the same speed, while expending less energy. Professional teams will often put their star rider behind another rider, allowing their star to expend less energy, saving for the final push of the race. Dividend investing is similar—you are using the dividends to draft off the stock, allowing your investment strategy to obtain similar returns, often with less risk.

CASE STUDY: CAROL AND DANIEL

Carol began investing in dividend-paying stocks at age 50 after a divorce left her responsible for both her retirement and the long-term care of her adult son, Daniel, who has a developmental disability.

Over the next 15 years, Carol focused on reinvesting all her dividends into a well-diversified portfolio of blue-chip dividend payers. By the time she retired at 65, that portfolio generated more than $32,000 annually in dividend income—enough to cover (when combined with her Social Security) much of her living expenses.

When Carol passed away at 82, the income stream continued—flowing into Daniel's third-party special needs trust. The trust used that income to support Daniel's hobbies, transportation, social outings, and even a modified van.

Because Carol built a reliable, self-sustaining stream of income, the need for additional life insurance was reduced. Her long-term planning gave Daniel the autonomy and joy she had always hoped for.

I hope you also see from this example that dividend investing is not for the super-rich only. Dividend investing can work across different wealth levels, providing access to a stream of income over multiple lifetimes.

THE PRINCIPLE OF COMPOUNDING: LET TIME DO THE WORK

Albert Einstein reportedly called compound interest the eighth wonder of the world—and for good reason. When you invest in dividend-paying companies and reinvest the income, you harness the power of compounding.

Let's break that down. You buy shares that pay dividends. Those dividends are reinvested to buy more shares. More shares lead to more dividends. The cycle repeats. Over time, this snowball effect can result in exponential growth—especially critical for families investing over two lifetimes.

This is also why we encourage families to not take only 12 months of returns as a comparison using dividend investing. When you look over periods of 10, 20, and 30 years, dividend investing emerges as a clear winner.

STRATEGY: REDUCE RISK WHILE BUILDING RELIABLE INCOME

A well-diversified dividend strategy can provide income to cover care costs and unexpected expenses, while reducing your exposure to sharp downturns. Families like Melinda and Katie don't just need retirement income—they need it to last another lifetime.

That means accomplishing the following:

- Building a core portfolio of dividend-paying companies
- Layering in fixed income or annuity options if appropriate
- Reducing sequence risk by avoiding unnecessary withdrawals during market downturns
- Ensuring reinvestment of income until needed

This strategy provides a buffer and creates flexibility, allowing families to respond to changes with more control and less stress.

FINAL THOUGHTS

Investing for two lifetimes requires a strategy that can weather market storms and deliver steady income. Dividend investing, when combined with growth and careful risk management, provides families with a durable foundation.

Families like Melinda's can rest easier knowing they have a plan to generate income for life, a strategy that supports their loved one long after they're gone, and a method that balances risk and growth.

We highly recommend you consult a financial planner/advisor who is familiar with special needs planning to analyze your portfolio—you don't have to do it alone. Your family deserves expert care and support.

Chapter 13

Self-care: Preserving Your Health, Identity, and Well-being

We often see our clients struggling to make time for and care for themselves. It's not unusual to hear about things normally considered errands, or tedious to other families, to be moments of relief for caregivers. That was evidenced when Kathy ran into one of our clients at the grocery store—the father of a young boy with debilitating anxiety. He mentioned he had a few minutes free while his wife was "covering" for him, so he was using the time to run errands. Our first thought is to feel sorrow that his only moment of respite was spent picking up groceries. But this dad was grateful for the break—no matter what it was.

This dad loves his son and is very devoted to him. And his son adores him. Let's be clear saying this: being a child plagued by debilitating anxiety is incredibly difficult. Being a caregiver of a child plagued by debilitating anxiety is also incredibly difficult. Finding opportunities for rest, relaxation, and respite—for both of them!—is extremely important. We say this because there has been backlash in the disability community when caregivers are painted as terrible when they complain about caregiving.

The reality is that communities are failing both people with disabilities *and* their caregivers. We need more support.

That being said, we can proactively support ourselves to be better caregivers and supporters of our children. Please know, there is no judgment if you are struggling with this right now. Perhaps it is an unusually hard season with lots of hospitalizations. Perhaps your usual support systems have dried up. We get it. And we encourage you—start taking some small steps to take care of yourself, to beef up your support system, and to find some respite. Self-care is critical—and it's often the first thing caregivers sacrifice.

How can families who provide constant care for a loved one with disabilities preserve their health, identity, and well-being? This chapter addresses the invisible toll caregiving takes on parents and siblings and gives practical guidance on how to build self-care, structure respite, and honor every family member's needs.

THE INVISIBLE TOLL OF CAREGIVING

Caregiving is something all parents and guardians do; it's part of the job. For families with disabilities, this job does not always have start and end times. We live with an inherent contrast: we want to care for our loved ones and have the specialized knowledge and tools to do it, and we also desire a break and to have some goals and dreams for ourselves. We know we need a break, but asking for a break seems selfish. And this vicious cycle goes on and on.

The first step is to have every family member go through the following exercise.

First, figure out what self-care actually means for them. For example, is it getting a massage once a week? Having a day off? Or maybe it's just making sure you get a chance to exercise or mediate. The point here is to take time for every family member to define what it means to them in an intentional way.

Maybe the term "self-care" is not meaningful to them—so use the language that works best for you! The goal is to find what activities leave them feeling rejuvenated.

We encourage you to think of not just one-off activities but things you can do intentionally, day after day and week after week. Maybe a massage once a month is enjoyable, but maybe they also need to be able to walk in the woods a few times a week and have 10 minutes every day put aside for some mindfulness and meditation.

Next is to think through what their needs are—emotionally, physically, and socially. For example, do you need to work out three times a week to de-stress? Each member should consider where their highest needs are. Is it needing emotional support, physical support, or social/community?

A therapist or supportive community such as a parent group can help address emotional support needs. Those seeking physical activity might think about taking a walk, joining a gym, or getting involved in a sport or regular routine. Those looking for community might find connection at church, or through growing their friendships. There are many ways to address your self-care, but the first place to start is knowing what you need and what supports or services might meet that need.

Now think about how to find time for the self-care, even in short bursts, for these activities. Sometimes we have to squeeze in rest time when we can find it. We have all had those days where we were lucky to do some intentional breathing on the way to work.

But by scheduling it and making it nonnegotiable, you can realize the benefits of self-care. And remember, quality over quantity! It is so important to make the time. You can start small, give yourself five minutes. Five quality minutes of self-care is better than the zero minutes you may currently have.

Some people make time before their loved one wakes up, just to sit and have a cup of coffee. Others might set up a regular arrangement with a paid caregiver to step in and provide an opportunity for more time. Focus more on getting started as opposed to waiting for an ideal time to present itself.

For those with children and adults with complex medical and support needs, it's also important to think through where to access respite services and support. We recognize that it may not be as easy as just hiring a babysitter through your local Facebook sitters group. Training a couple of family members or close friends who are willing to give you a few hours a week is a great place to start. Even if you don't have a plan of what to do, using the time to have them practice the caregiving is a great way to get started.

If this is feeling overwhelming, this is something we help parents with all the time as part of our overall special needs planning support. Know that you are not alone, and we can help.

Respite services, which we describe in more detail later in this chapter, can be provided through Medicaid waiver services, through local agencies that provide in-home care, and through nonprofit organizations. Be sure to see what is available in your area in order to choose the right option for you, and if you don't see it, ask. Sometimes, particularly in rural areas or under-resourced areas, there can be an absence of services in general. In these instances, it is important to connect with others in your community to see what you can do together or how you can advocate for change.

We talked with a group of parents who set aside one day a month to come together in a park with their loved ones to share in community together and build relationships, meeting their social and emotional self-care needs. We have seen other small towns come together to provide a community center where families could come together and support each other. Once they rented the building for the community center, they were able to gather other supports and grants for their community. It was truly an "if you build it, they will come" moment.

Counselors or therapists (for emotional support) can be a great resource for caregivers. They can help you find ways you can care for yourself, provide you with tools to handle the stress of caregiving, and help you process trauma related to your child.

Counselors and therapists can be found through your health insurance provider, talking with your trusted doctor, or by asking your friends and community who they recommend, if you feel comfortable asking. Make sure you know how they're paid, if they accept insurance, and what their policies are for canceled appointments. You may also want to ask about whether they meet virtually or in person.

Most importantly, if you are meeting with a counselor or therapist and you feel they are not a good fit, do not feel like this is a marriage. You can find another person with the same qualifications who may be a better fit for you. I always recommend you treat it like dating. Make sure you find someone that you are comfortable doing the hard work of delving into trauma.

And here is another thing to think about. Therapy can be a really important self-care. But you may need something light that is enjoyable in the moment to do to offset the heaviness you delve into in therapy.

Life coaches or mentors can also be helpful for goal setting and to get some help with setting your own goals (or anyone in your family who uses them). Some parents become so focused on caregiving that it becomes difficult to remember what their own interests and goals are. A life coach or mentor can help them rediscover their passions or find new ones.

Life coaches and mentors have grown in popularity, particularly as people look to structure and change their day-to-day lives. Life coaches are professionals so you will want to make sure you vet available providers and check references.

We also know many people with disabilities who fall on the "in-between" area—not medically complex, but not able to fully function on their own—who are able to engage life coaches to help them put processes in place that will increase their independence. These individuals are often experienced at doing exactly this—helping people with disabilities increase independence—and can either supplement personal care attendants or sometimes replace them entirely.

Mentors, on the other hand, are usually people who have a similar life experience or who can provide guidance as a result of their own experience or training. They can often be found through friends, through your religious groups such as churches and synagogues, and through nonprofit organizations. Some state departments that provide mental health and disability services also often provide mentorship programs for parents and caregivers. These can be a great resource!

Medicaid waiver caseworkers or care managers can be another great avenue to access respite services. Your Medicaid case manager is usually going to be found through your local office for disability services or social services. Since every state administers these programs differently, you will need to determine which office in your state offers this service. Case managers are in place to assist individuals and families to navigate programs and services.

You may also consider family facilitators to help balance needs among family members. Family facilitators can be found through therapy programs, psychological services, or family service providers. Your local community services board or family doctor would be a good person to ask about local providers in your area. Family facilitators are sometimes called family coaches. In general, they will meet with your entire family and will take direction from you on what aspects you would like to see improvement on or helping you communicate more effectively. For example, a family facilitator may help train the family on how to avoid triggering situations for members of the family who have difficulty with emotional regulation. They can help with family routines, and they can help those who may communicate differently to express their needs to the family.

Obviously, we don't want you to think these are the only types of professionals available to support you. These are just some categories that we say our families using frequently.

SELF-CARE ISN'T ALWAYS WHAT YOU THINK

When people hear "self-care," they often think of hobbies, spa days, or creative outlets. But for caregivers, self-care might be much more basic—and that's okay.

Self-care might also be attending your own medical, dental, or therapy appointments. We hear too often from caregivers who have put their own needs last—not doing their annual physical, getting regular dental cleanings, or seeking help to process their own complex emotions around caregiving and their own lives.

And here is one of our personal favorite types of self-care: taking a shower without being interrupted. Do you have a big, beautiful bathtub whose job is basically to look pretty because it's never used? We do, and it's not because we don't like baths. There never seems to be the opportunity for us to escape while everyone is home.

We've even asked for our big present from our family to be a day in our home by ourselves. Peace, quiet, ability to take a bath, veg on the couch, and just do nothing in our own space. There's nothing quite like it—being in your own home, where you can wear the comfiest robe, put a face mask on, and not have any demands. (Of course, as caregivers, we must then work hard to not get distracted and start doing a load of laundry or stress cleaning.)

Some days, your self-care might be as simple as drinking your coffee while it's still hot. Dr. Becky had a whole initiative during COVID-19 where she encouraged parents to give themselves the time to sit and drink a hot cup of coffee. It resonated with millions of parents across the United States who were struggling with the stress of working from home while caregiving. For parents of special needs children—no matter their age—that stress is omnipresent.

You're getting the idea now: meditating for five minutes, enjoying a pastry in silence, or reading a book during your lunch instead of multitasking by sitting on hold with your insurance company.

And here is another thing you can do: strategically spend in a way that you can outsource as much as you can afford. Take a look at your budget and see if there are places where you can save or cut expenses in areas that are not bringing you great joy, while spending in areas that can help reduce your mental load: hire a housekeeper to help with cleaning and tidying, order groceries instead of going to the store. You get the idea.

In our households, we are now starting to add some of these tasks back in as we work to teach our kids how to do these necessary items that we want them to learn and know how to do. Whether you outsource during a particularly difficult period, or indefinitely, let go of the guilt, and accept that many areas of your life are hard, and this doesn't have to be one of them. It's okay to not be superman/woman.

Some families provide round-the-clock care. In those homes, self-care might feel like a luxury—or even a source of guilt. But it shouldn't be. If all you managed today was to stay hydrated or get your favorite coffee during a hospital stay—that's worth celebrating.

Caregiver stress levels have been shown to rival those of individuals in high-endurance sports training. Realistic self-care is about listening to your body and taking what's available in the moment.

SELF-CARE IN ACTION: A THREE-STEP PROCESS

Now that you know what self-care is and isn't, here is an action plan to get you started. This details how to identify your needs and goals, how to schedule and execute your self-care plan, and how to find like-minded people and community.

1. Identify Your Needs and Goals

    If you've been caregiving for years, you might not even know what self-care looks like. You may need professional help to explore interests, identify stress points, and set goals—just like you might do in person-centered planning for your child.

2. Schedule and Execute

    Put it on the calendar. Whether it's a walk, a support group meeting, or 10 minutes to breathe—treat it like a doctor's appointment. Enlist others to help make it happen.

3. Find Your People

    Connect with other caregivers. They'll get it. They'll understand that 10 minutes of uninterrupted time is a win. These connections are your fuel. And if someone has the nerve to start talking to you about how if you just meal planned your life would be easier, or how not exercising is a choice, well, they just don't get it. Find your people—they're out there, and they will get it. Look on Eventbrite, Meetup, and Facebook for events and get togethers. We have found Facebook groups to be the best way to meet other parents.

GETTING MORE OFFICIAL SELF-CARE: RESPITE

Respite is short-term relief for primary caregivers, allowing someone else to temporarily take over caregiving duties so you can rest. Medicaid waivers, local nonprofits, and community programs often provide these services.

It's time to rest, reconnect, and refuel. We understand that it can seem difficult—sometimes impossible—to find a trusted caregiver that you can leave your medically complex or behaviorally needy child with, especially because we have all heard the horror stories of abuse.

We work with some families who have not taken a vacation for more than 20 years. There is no easy solution here. It is doubtful that if you have not been on a vacation and have trouble trusting providers that you will make one phone call, find the perfect person, and leave for a vacation with no anxiety (although we do wish that for you!).

The reality will likely be a multistep process. Be prepared to break it down into steps. Start by doing your homework when looking at respite providers. Make sure any paid providers you use have background checks and references. As discussed further in this chapter, organizations that facilitate respite will have a process regarding how providers are hired and onboarded. Make sure you take the time to understand their process.

Start talking to your child in language or ways that they can understand about small steps coming up. Go out for an afternoon. Then make it a day trip. Expand it to an overnight. Then try for a full weekend—in a hotel in town.

Other organizations such as your local nonprofits and companies such as those that offer access to paid babysitters are other great places to check as well. If your child has a friend or a trusted adult, see if they would participate in the respite with them (or at least part of it). If you have a microboard, share with them what your goals are.

And don't overlook family members. Maybe you've been reluctant to ask for help, feeling that they don't know the steps involved in providing care. Take the time to train your family members. And use all the tools at your disposal to help. Your microboard can aid in this process as well.

Parents who have never left their children with anyone, never had time for themselves, and their children are unable to travel tell us that home starts to feel like a prison. They feel angry and resentful.

There are options with respite, and it is important to find these opportunities not only for parents to get the rest and time for themselves that they require as humans, but also for their children to develop the ability to go through their normal routines without parents there. It will be a necessary skill to have for when parents are no longer able to care for their children as they age. Do this for you—and for them. Respite gives you the space to take care of yourself, not just errands.

CASE STUDY: THE THOMPSON FAMILY

Care plans often revolve around the person with a disability—but every family member has needs. Let's take a look at the Thompson family. Bob and Lynda are in their 60s, providing full-time care to Jack, who is 32, has autism, and lives with

Case Study: The Thompson Family

them. James (30) is Jack's brother and is married with two kids. Bob and Lynda not only care for Jack but also are the primary childcare providers to James' two kids, who are 4 and 6.

Bob is currently working, but he wants to retire and help Lynda, who feels overstretched. He also would like a deeper connection to his grandkids and the ability to go to more of their sporting events. Lynda is feeling the need to "retire" as well—and wants to encourage James to hire an additional caregiver so that she is not the only one filling in when James and his wife need to work late. But she is afraid to say anything because she knows how hard James and his wife work and how important their careers are to them. They also work hard because they know that one day they will be caring for Jack—who needs round-the-clock care.

And Jack, well, Jack wants everything to stay exactly the same. He has a lot of trouble adapting to his niece and nephew being over at the house more when summer comes around.

A sudden health change in Bob or Lynda could collapse this structure. Planning ahead—with paid caregivers, respite options, and emergency plans—can prevent crises. James and his wife are not only in the sandwich generation but could find themselves caring for three generations at the same time—Bob and Lynda, Jack, and their own children as well. A plan for their respite as well as a plan for how Bob, Lynda, and Jack will be able to engage other caregivers is absolutely necessary for the well-being of the entire family.

We often talk about person-centered planning for individuals with disabilities, but families thrive when every person is considered. Maybe Bob wants to take a cruise. With a bit of planning—such as respite coverage for Jack and backup childcare for James' family—that dream becomes possible.

FINAL THOUGHTS

If you are reading this and still wondering where to start, we encourage you to begin with some questions. What does each family member want? What is their capacity to help? What are their dreams?

Asking about dreams and planning as a family to achieve them lifts every member up. And planning together in this way helps to put the support in place and to acknowledge to every member, we are all important and we can help each other.

Families who prioritize self-care become more resilient. By integrating respite, acknowledging every family member's needs, and setting goals—big and small—they create a more sustainable caregiving journey.

Self-care isn't selfish. It's the fuel that keeps the whole plan running.

Chapter 14

Relax and Enjoy

Let's face it—caregiving can take over everything. But a joyful life, even with significant caregiving responsibilities, is still possible. This chapter is a reminder: joy, connection, and recreation are not luxuries. They're necessities.

Whether you love travel, cooking, music, or movement, it's important to make space for hobbies and shared family experiences—no matter how big or small.

Families can and do make time for joy when their daily lives are full of caregiving responsibilities. This chapter focuses on creating space for leisure, travel, and recreation. Exploring how hobbies and exercise improve well-being. And supporting family identity and individual interests. If we can do this, you can too.

CASE STUDY: THE OLIVEIRA FAMILY

The Oliveiras are a close-knit family with two children: 10-year-old Mateo, who has Turner syndrome and requires round-the-clock support, and his older sister, Ana, 16 years old. The entire family loves to travel—but traveling with Mateo hasn't always been easy. Transitions are hard for him, unfamiliar places can cause distress, and changes to routine often trigger meltdowns.

But Ana had a dream: she wanted the family to visit Portugal, as she'd been learning Portuguese in school. Over the course of two years, she saved her birthday money and earnings from a small online craft shop she started. She even researched the language, culture, and geography to help plan the trip.

The entire family got involved. Mateo's therapists worked on small daily changes to build his flexibility. The family did short practice trips: day outings, overnight stays, new restaurants. They slowly built his ability to tolerate—and enjoy—new experiences.

When the time came, the trip to Portugal was a success. They found an amusement park for Mateo—who loves roller coasters. His joy became the highlight of the trip. The parents found a restaurant that offered an early seating with a private dining room, giving Mateo the calm setting he needed. Ana's language skills helped the family connect with locals and navigate smoothly.

Was it perfect? No. But it was meaningful. It was connection. And it proved that shared joy is worth planning for.

HOW TO RELAX AND ENJOY

Relaxing and enjoying life is something many of us take for granted. As parents and caregivers of children with disabilities, relaxing and enjoying life can be in conflict with daily caregiving. It may be hard to imagine and maybe even something you feel you don't deserve. You might feel that taking time to indulge a bit is somehow leaving your loved one out or taking time away from them. We feel you can have both! The first goal is finding that joy and determining how to realize it.

Start by focusing on what brings each person joy. This is a great exercise for each member of the family. Take time to identify and discuss and share. You might even make it into a fun family game: *Pictionary*, where you are guessing what the other person is drawing about what they enjoy.

Maybe for one member, it's getting the chance to golf on Saturday mornings. Maybe for another member, it's weekly horseback riding. It could even be more simple; you might find that your loved one enjoys walks, and maybe it's time that turns into a regular family affair in the evenings or on the weekend. Whether it's riding bikes, family ski trips, or going out on a boat, it can be as simple or as big as you'd like. Whatever it is, take time to identify those activities that bring each person joy.

Now think about what activities or routines can become shared hobbies. Just as the previous walking idea, can any of the individual joys turn into opportunities for shared activities? Maybe if one member finds joy in gardening, there is a way for others to get involved. Maybe another joy is bike riding, and you can find a way for everyone to join in. Find an adaptive bicycle or a trailer and see if there are some trails in your town.

If you are having trouble figuring out how to make an activity into a family activity, take some time together to think of what the barriers are. Some may be harder to overcome (taking a sensory sensitive adult to a loud concert may be a no go), but others may have simpler solutions. For example, we had a family in which the father enjoyed bike riding, but he felt guilty going out for a ride while the others stayed home. They decided to make it a priority each weekend to take the bike with them to the park so that he could ride while the others played. This way, his joy turned into a shared activity.

Travel is an activity that we hear often is a challenge and is something that families would really like to learn how to enjoy. The first step to accessing travel for your family is knowing what the barriers are for you.

In general, accessibility has improved in many ways over the years. There are many parks and experiences that now have accessibility options, sensory friendly spaces, and that provide bypasses to long wait lines. Airlines are also offering supports and prioritized boarding for people with disabilities, as well as ways to prepare for travel ahead of time, to address any anxiety or potential challenges. The bottom line, think about where you want to go and ask how your loved one's needs can be supported.

Take some time and think about what items can you bring with you to make the new destination feel like home. Think about special treats, well-loved items, and safe foods that may make the trip easier. We know some families bring kraft macaroni and cheese with them to the hotel so that their child has something safe to eat while they are traveling because food is the biggest barrier for them. Others let their kids travel while wearing pajamas and noise canceling headphones. Some airports will do "practice days" where they allow people with disabilities to come and practice the process of going through security and boarding an airplane. Visual schedules and other therapeutic tools can also be a huge help!

As your thinking about tools, think about the supports that will make recreation sustainable for you. What tools will help your family have a more enjoyable time? When Kristin and her family went to Disneyland, they rented adaptive strollers. While her children don't have specific mobility issues, they lack the strength and coordination to last in a whole day of walking and also benefitted from being able to close the stroller off, put their headphones on, and retreat from the sensory overwhelm. That one little detail took planning: knowing what Disney's requirements were to allow adaptive strollers in the park, what company would rent the stroller, and how to get it delivered.

From fidgets to extra battery chargers for tablets/phones/computers, it will be worth it to take the extra time to bring the things needed to make the time successful. With a little work, and patience, you can have success.

PRACTICAL TOOLS AND WHO CAN HELP

As you plan to embark on your relaxation and enjoyment journey, you may want to consider engaging a professional. Rather than avoiding or putting it off, a professional can help assess your individual situation and provide recommendations. People who regularly work in the disability space such as occupational therapists, behavior analysts, and other providers get it. They see the challenges every day. It can help to lean into their supports and services as you take the next step.

Occupational therapists may not be who you think of first in getting help with recreational activities, but we have found them to be extremely helpful in problem solving and helping finding solutions for families in finding activities that work for all—and putting a plan in place to support the family in reaching their goals. They can help by assessing the individual's needs, identify and recommend adaptive equipment, teach individuals with disabilities how to prepare, and help to manage daily activities. An occupational therapist (OT) can also help to break your plan into segments, introducing the process slowly, without going quickly to the end goal.

For example, they might suggest first putting together a visual story of your activity, then going online and looking at pictures of what the venue looks like, then driving there together but not going in, and then going but for a very short time. OTs can also be up front with you if they think something is not achievable or you should look in a different direction. Helicopter skiing may not be an achievable goal, but adaptive skiing at a place that offers that service may be a great and achievable compromise.

Behavior analysts can be another great professional to prepare your family for new experiences. Behavior analysts can help address any potential challenges that arise due to a change in routine; can help to identify supports such as schedules, routines, and strategies to increase engagement; and can help coach parents and caregivers on how to support their loved one's needs as they transition and activities change around them. One of the greatest benefits of a behavior analyst is that they may think of details that will impact your success that you had not thought of because they are trained to look at the surroundings and see how they impact behavior and then try adjustments.

Some OTs and behavior analysists will provide family or parent coaching. If this is a service you are interested in, be sure to ask them first if they provide it, and second if it is covered by insurance or if you will need to pay out of pocket. Surprise out-of-pocket expenses are never fun for anyone!

Travel coaches or special needs travel consultants also exist! Some people are trained or experienced in helping to plan and organize trips for people with disabilities. Some organizations even offer solo trips for people with disabilities, with full support! Their services may include planning the trip, assisting with accessible accommodations, arranging transportation, customizing itineraries, and helping to ensure the comfort and safety of the person with a disability.

We have also seen some inclusive travel destinations pop up—cruise lines that specialize in working with autistic families; Autism of the Seas and Morgan's Wonderland in Texas are a few. Some entrepreneurs have children with disabilities or are disabled themselves and recognize the need for disability friendly vacations.

One family we work with bought a Marriott timeshare because every Marriot location around the world is wheelchair accessible. Another family arranges trips where dad (who doesn't particularly like travel) stays home with the two kids who also prefer being home, while mom travels with the three kids that enjoy travel. Later in the chapter we will give some more tips on places that are disability friendly and offer extra supports.

Support groups can be a great way to trade stories and share solutions. Other families may have tips and tricks to share—especially local ones!—that worked for them. Engaging with a support group of like-minded people can help you to not only share in your experience but to also hear the successes of others. We are all in this together, and we all have had our ups and downs. Sharing what works and what resources have been the most helpful can be extremely valuable.

Developing both family-wide and individual hobbies is essential and a great way to relax and enjoy. You might try creating a family "fun list" of affordable activities everyone enjoys, rotating choices between family members to ensure each person's interests are represented. You might also try exploring accessible community events and inclusive recreation options.

Keep in mind that in the beginning, when it is new, the activity might not be enjoyable for anyone. It may take more time and effort than you feel you want to spend. Only you can say if it's worth it. We encourage you to lead with hope and then reevaluate along the way. If the activity never gets to be enjoyable for your family, then switch course.

The goal is to get your family to a place where you have hobbies and activities that can be done for years, decades, and generations.

CASE STUDY: THE CHUNG FAMILY

The Chung family includes parents Min and Lily, their 15-year-old Sophie, who has autism, and 12-year-old Lucas, who has Down syndrome. Rather than focusing on one single family activity, each member of the family pursues their own interests—with support from the others and their broader special needs community.

Lucas participates in Special Olympics year-round, where he's made friends and thrives with regular structure. Sophie is passionate about contemporary dance and recently joined a community dance troupe that includes neurodiverse members. Lily tends to their backyard garden, which has grown into a beautiful space filled with vegetables, wildflowers, and a tiny greenhouse. Meanwhile, Min connects with other dads every Sunday to watch football, sharing snacks and stories while their kids play nearby. And every year they take a cruise on Autism of the Seas, a tradition that the entire family looks forward to every year. They have made friends with other families who now plan for the same week and go together, and everyone keeps in touch via email and Facetime during the year. Lucas has a countdown calendar to the week they'll take the trip, and Sophie helps him cross each day off and keep track of how many days are left until they leave.

These activities aren't just hobbies—they're lifelines. The Chungs have created a rhythm that respects each person's individuality while reinforcing a sense of collective support.

ADAPTIVE TRAVEL DESTINATIONS

Some destinations go above and beyond in creating inclusive experiences. This list is not exhaustive, and the other thing to keep in mind is what your family's unique needs are and whether these places can/do accommodate them. What works for one family may not work for another.

Here are a few places we recommend:

> **Dollywood:** Offers accessibility guides and ride accommodations. We have had many families attend who reported back how supported they felt at Dollywood. It's also a smaller park and does not tend to have the same crowds as larger theme parks. If Disneyland or Disneyworld is your ultimate goal, Dollywood may be a great place to start. Check out more information at dollywood.com.
> **Legoland:** Known for sensory-friendly events and disability access services. This is a great opportunity, especially for kiddos who really enjoy playing with Legos, for the family to go and feel supported. Check out legoland.com.

Disney Parks: Disney offers the Disability Access Service (DAS) to reduce wait times and provide accommodations. While the process to get the DAS pass may feel like you are jumping through a lot of hoops, Disney does a phenomenal job of accommodating those with disabilities. From sensory spaces to recharge, adaptive strollers available to rent, wheelchair adaptive costumes, and staff who are trained on how to spot a meltdown and assist a struggling parent/caregiver, many families return to Disney year after year. The rides are also available to be viewed on YouTube for people who would benefit from seeing them ahead of time. Go to disney.com for more information.

Morgan's Wonderland: A fully accessible theme park designed by a father for his daughter with special needs. This theme park is a water park where every feature is fully accessible and thought through. This theme park is gaining in popularity as those around the world flock to experience a water park that their whole family can enjoy. Check out morganswonderland.org.

Autism on the Seas Cruises: Specialized cruises with support staff and accommodations for families with autism. We have talked to families that have gone on these cruises, and behavior analysts volunteer every year to help families have a fun and accessible vacation. All say it's an incredible experience where you are surrounded by people who "get it" and are ready to jump in and help. Autismontheseas.com has more information.

MOVEMENT AND EXERCISE FOR ALL ABILITIES

Besides travel, consider ways to relax and enjoy through movement. Whether it is walking, biking, swimming, jumping on the trampoline, whatever it is for you and your family, it is important to incorporate it regularly.

Exercise can and should be accessible for everyone. Adaptive exercise recognizes the reality that all bodies—regardless of ability—benefit from movement. Whether someone has cerebral palsy, uses a wheelchair, has low muscle tone, or experiences coordination challenges, there are tailored movement routines and activities that can improve health, resilience, and emotional well-being.

We love that in NICUs and PICUs across the country, physical therapists are starting to work with doctors and nurses to find how to incorporate movement within medical treatment—navigating monitors, wires, IVs, to help babies and children experience movement. It is no surprise that this is leading to happier babies and children, and we believe future research will show this provides better outcomes for all.

Movement also supports individuals with sensory processing differences. For sensory-seeking individuals, rhythmic and high-energy movement may bring a sense of calm or regulation. We know some sensory seekers enjoy the deep input of weight-lifting, running, and other deep input activities. These can also help calm their nervous system in a safe way, without having to seek bigger (unsafe) thrills. For sensory-avoidant individuals, gentle stretching or mindful yoga might offer a grounding experience.

Beyond physical benefits, movement can regulate mood and reduce anxiety, support better sleep, and build confidence and independence. What's more, movement can create opportunities for social connection. We hear from many adults with intellectual disability that the Special Olympics is their favorite social outlet. This is no surprise: movement and socializing just go together.

Did you know that movement can also help you learn a new skill faster? So, if your loved one is struggling to learn a new skill, try incorporating a small movement with it. Whether it's a jump, a hand motion, or a favorite dance movement, try pairing the movement with the skill and see what happens.

Small, consistent efforts count. Five minutes of movement is better than none. Adaptive sports, inclusive dance, accessible gyms, and even at-home routines can all be powerful tools to support long-term health and happiness.

CREATING JOY ON A BUDGET

We talked about traveling, hobbies, exercise, and so much more. But if you are avoiding these activities due to financial strain or limited resources, we have several suggestions for you too.

Look out for free or low-cost community programs, parks, or libraries. Community programs can be found through your local community service board or local nonprofits that offer regular opportunities to explore or come together for enjoyment. Also take time to identify your local parks and libraries. They too often have events and special activities which can be enjoyable for every member of your family.

Maybe you live in an area that doesn't have as many community options. Don't let that stop you! Start a backyard garden or an indoor plant project. The COVID-19 pandemic ignited lots of new stay-at-home ideas focused on bringing the fun to your own backyard. Websites and apps such as Etsy, Pinterest, and Reddit offer lots of ideas for DIY projects and activities that can be adapted to every member of the family—and provide some beauty inside and outside of your home.

Try some family art nights or cooking new meals together. A favorite for the Carletons is to find trash and items laying around the house to make art. Most recently they've been making playgrounds and reimagining what their favorite playgrounds would look like if it had all the features they enjoy. The only tools needed are scissors and glue!

And last, sometimes penciling in a new activity can go a long way. Make a family calendar and tell everyone ahead of time what's coming. Talk about who will be involved and what you will be doing. Make a big deal about a new pack of *Uno* cards coming in the mail—"This is for family game night! I'm going to put it in our new game night spot." Ask everyone what food they'd like to have during the activity. You don't need to plan too far ahead. Just making the time is the first step; the rest will follow.

FINAL THOUGHTS

You deserve joy. So does your child. So does every member of your family.

It's not about being able to afford big trips or having more time than other people—it's about making space for joy, however it fits into your life. One moment of laughter, one shared story, one memory made—these are the things we carry.

Start where you are. Plan with intention. And allow yourself the grace to relax, enjoy, and be fully present.

Chapter 15

Planning for Military Families

Families who serve in the military face unique challenges, and those challenges can multiply when a child has a disability. But the military also provides unique opportunities—benefits that, when understood and properly applied for, can offer powerful lifetime support. This chapter outlines how military families can secure long-term financial and medical stability for their child with special needs.

In this chapter, we walk you through military retirement and survivor pension planning, TRICARE for Life and DEERS registration, and how to ensure your military benefits don't jeopardize your child's public benefits.

As a team, we want to thank every person who has served in our military and supported our freedoms. We appreciate your sacrifice, especially and including those who have disabled children and have navigated the sacrifice of service along with the challenge of raising a child with a lifelong disability. Thank you, from the bottom of our hearts.

Now, let's look at planning—and help you begin to understand what we know is a complicated process.

CASE STUDY: THE THOMPSONS' PLAN FOR LIFELONG SUPPORT

Sgt. Michael Thompson and his spouse, Carla, have a 22-year-old son, Ethan, who has intellectual and developmental disabilities. Ethan has aged out of the school system and participates in a Medicaid waiver day program. He is also a disabled adult child (DAC) collecting Social Security benefits based on his father's work record. Michael is about to retire from military service and is reviewing his survivor benefits.

With help from their special needs financial planner (who was also familiar with military planning), the Thompsons confirmed that Ethan could receive Michael's military survivor pension benefit—but only if he was correctly listed as a dependent with special needs and a first-party special needs trust (SNT) was submitted to DFAS (Defense Finance and Accounting Service). They updated Ethan's DEERS (Defense Enrollment Eligibility Reporting System) record, submitted the trust documentation, and now have confidence that Ethan will receive both his DAC benefit and a military pension for life—plus health coverage through TRICARE for Life.

This planning didn't just ensure that Ethan will be well cared for—it also took immense pressure off Michael and Carla's investment assets and the need for additional life insurance. With their Social Security and savings, Michael and Carla were on track for their own retirement budget and now had peace of mind for Ethan.

GETTING MILITARY BENEFITS

Military families often don't realize how much planning must be done to ensure their child remains eligible for critical benefits. From ensuring proper survivor designation to creating a first-party trust and navigating DEERS and DFAS requirements, the system is complex—but it's worth it.

As with any system, there are specific terms and acronyms. Let's go through a few here:

DEERS: Defense Enrollment Eligibility Reporting System

- DEERS is a Department of Defense (DoD) database that identifies and verifies individuals such as military sponsors, their family members, and certain civilians, who are eligible for DoD benefits, primarily TRICARE health benefits, and military ID cards.
- Sponsors are automatically enrolled in DEERS.
- Sponsors register eligible family members.
- Be sure to keep DEERS information up to date.

DFAS: Defense Finance and Accounting Service

- DFAS is a DoD agency responsible for providing financial and accounting services, including payroll, vendor payments, and managing payments to military personnel, retirees, and civilians.
- DFAS provides payroll.
- It manages and pays military retirees and their survivors as well as other financial services to the military and its vendors.

The military system can seem overwhelming, but its benefits to sponsors and their families are significant and worth taking the time to understand in order to be sure you are taking advantage of the right benefits. There are specific requirements and procedures that are important to know and follow, and you should stay aware as they change or get updated.

We hear many families say that they would prefer to rely on their own investments or insurance. And we understand—many families prefer to feel they are doing this on our own. We encourage you to sit down with an experienced special needs financial planner so that you can see in-depth what your options are—and how each different option may impact your child's livelihood. While systems may change, we always recommend making the best decision that you can with the data you have available. If you do not explore all the data/options, you will not be able to make an informed decision.

> **NOTE:** Many military benefits come at lower cost and fees than private sector or civilian benefits. Knowing your options is the key to making an informed decision.

That's one of the reasons we wrote this book. Education should be available to all families. While we may not know your particular circumstances, we aim to provide you with a framework to be able to fill in your own personal details—and then seek advice when you feel you have enough education.

DEERS AND TRICARE FOR MILITARY FAMILIES

We mentioned above what DEERS is—the first step for a military family is to make sure that your child with a disability is enrolled in DEERS. This system tracks benefits like TRICARE and may also come with benefits like allowing your child to access military bases to be able to use the commissary and post exchange. Sometimes this access can result in steep discounts to what is available outside of bases and can be a great benefit.

TRICARE has been mentioned a few times, and we want to make sure to explain it fully. TRICARE is a federal health benefits program. It provides comprehensive healthcare coverage for both active-duty service members, retirees, and families. TRICARE can be a phenomenal resource because it can provide access to both the Military Health System (MHS) as well as a network of civilian healthcare providers. The network is vast, and those we speak to in the military say that access to TRICARE is a phenomenal benefit for their family.

Normally, TRICARE is available until age 21 (or age 23 if enrolled in college/university). However, for an adult child of a military service member (or retiree) who is deemed incapacitated, TRICARE for life can be available for their lifetime as well. There are some steps that you must follow in order to make sure that your child remains eligible for TRICARE for life.[1]

The child must remain unmarried and dependent on the service member for support. There must be an incapacity determination completed. The DoD uses the term "incapacitated child," or "secondary dependency"—meaning, someone who is unable to support themselves due to a mental or physical condition. They also must have been determined incapacitated before age 18 or have become incapacitated before the age of 21 (or 23 if enrolled in college/university). The child must be dependent on the service member (called sponsor in DoD language) or retiree for more than 50% of their support or have been dependent on them for more than 50% of support at the time of the service member's death.

When applying for TRICARE for life, you will need to have a few documents on hand. The first is a medical sufficiency statement. The medical sufficiency statement should be done by your child's primary care physician and should include details such as diagnosis, date of onset of the condition (which would be birth if it is a congenital or chromosomal condition), level of incapacitation, and capability of self-support. The physical must also state if the incapacitation is expected to be permanent. The statement or letter should be completed and dated within 90 days of the application.

You will also need DD Form 137-5 (found on the Defense Finance and Accounting Service website), filled out and notarized, to show financial dependency. Both of these documents will need to be resubmitted every four years. This will be needed not only to keep TRICARE but also to keep their military ID card.

There are slightly different processes for submitting this documentation depending on which branch of the military the sponsor served in. We recommend that you go to the Department of Finance and Accounting Service website (DFAS) to find the current full details for which branch of service you were in.[2] At the time of publication, each branch required the forms mentioned previously.

It is important to know that TRICARE can serve as primary or secondary insurance, depending on the insurance plan. Most often, it serves as secondary insurance—alongside Medicare, private insurance plans, employer offered insurance plans, and more. However, alongside Medicaid, TRICARE pays first.

Let's summarize why TRICARE for Life matters. It functions similarly to a Medicare supplement policy and is available for life to disabled dependents who meet eligibility. It can be used as primary or secondary insurance, it covers a broad range of medical expenses including therapies and prescriptions, and it remains in place even after the military parent passes, as long as proper registration and documentation are maintained. TRICARE for Life can be coordinated with Medicare and Medicaid, providing robust healthcare coverage and reducing the need for out-of-pocket expenses.

PENSION ANALYSIS

Once you have submitted these forms and obtained TRICARE for Life, let's talk about what to do if you are eligible for a military pension based on your service. The first thing we want you to do is go to the Military OneSource website and use its online calculator to determine what your military retirement benefits or pension will be.[3] You can also go to the DoD and go through its series of calculations to calculate your pension.[4] If you started your service in the military after 1986, you will be eligible for its dual retirement system: access to the Thrift Savings Plan as well as a pension.

The great news is that your estimate will likely be lower than what you will actually receive because the military offers annual COLA (cost of living adjustments) to military pensions, meaning if the cost of living has been determined to increase, the amount you receive for your pension will go up by that amount. This makes military pensions better than many annuities that you can purchase privately because inflation protection is built in.

Now that you have calculated your pension, let's talk about the Survivor Benefit Program (SBP). The SBP is designed to allow a military retiree to choose to provide a remainder benefit in the form of a continuous lifetime annuity to their dependents. In plain language, the eligible retired service member can choose to leave a percentage of their pension to their spouse and children either under the age of 18 or deemed as incapacitated for their lifetime.

A retiree pays the premium for this benefit out of their pension income, pre-tax. This is important because it means they don't count as income, leading to paying less tax and less out-of-pocket cost. The premiums are supplemented by the government, and the cost of running the program is paid entirely by the government. This is the primary reason that when comparisons are done of survivor benefit pensions to privately funded/obtained annuities, the SBP is almost always the clear winner.

It is important to know that the SBP goes in the following order: spouse first, and then if/when spouse passes away, then to the children/disabled adult children. This means that you will have to wait until your spouse has passed away for your child to start receiving the SBP. Additionally, the SBP is for 55% of the amount of the retiree's pension.

Now let's talk about the steps you will want to consider taking to take advantage of the SBP. The first step is on that was mentioned earlier: your dependent child must be properly listed in DEERS as permanently disabled.

Next, contact DFAS and determine what the fee is that you will need to pay to access the SBP. Compare that fee to other annuity options. We recommend that you do this with the help of a special needs financial planner. You can do it on your own, but it is much easier with financial planning software and easier access to annuity companies. You can also compare the fee to putting that money into a life insurance policy and see how much life insurance you would receive compared to the lifelong annuity.

Of course, another important part of choosing the SBP is making sure that you can afford the fee and that it will not cause undue hardship to your family. Take a look at your budget and all of your sources of income. Check to see if you could afford to either take the income from other assets, or if you can live on the lower income (after paying the fee).

You only need to read this next part if you have decided that the SBP is the right choice for your family. If it is, then there are several more steps that you should take. Notate if your child that you are planning for is either utilizing currently or is expected to utilize in the future government benefits. This is another decision that we encourage you to make with a professional. Make sure that you have your cost of care handy and have a good working knowledge of the benefits available and if your child would qualify. If the answer to these questions is yes, you will want to take steps to protect their access to these benefits while also collecting the SBP.

DFAS has worked with CMS (the Center for Medicare and Medicaid Services) to allow the SBP to be paid to a first-party SNT. The reason it needs to be a first-party trust is that the pension is paid to the individual, not a third party, so the money is considered first party. This was done by exception and is considered a privilege, so Medicaid will still be looking for a payback once the beneficiary/disabled dependent has passed away. An estate planner familiar with military special needs planning is highly recommended. At the least, you will want to work with an elder law attorney. You need to make sure that you have not only the trust but certification of the trust, and you will need to establish a tax ID for the trust. The tax ID can be obtained from the IRS and can be done by you, your attorney, a CPA, or other competent individual.

Once the trust is complete, you will need to make sure you have elected spouse and child, or child only, with DFAS. Next, gather all of your documentation. You will need a written statement of your decision to have the annuity paid to the SNT, an attorney's special needs trust certification,[5] and the name and tax ID number for the SNT by or before the time your beneficiary applies for their annuity.

You are now ready to submit the paperwork to DFAS! You can submit through their online portal by going to their website and clicking on "Retirees and Annuitants,"[6] you can mail the documents to:

> Defense Finance and Accounting Service
> U.S. Military Retired Pay
> 8899 E 56th Street
> Indianapolis, IN 46249-1200
> Or you can fax to 1-800-469-6559.

If the retiree had chosen the spouse and child option but has not submitted the required documentation to have it paid to an SNT, it's not too late! Any surviving parent, grandparent, or court-appointed legal guardian may make the designation on behalf of the incapacitated individual.

- Once completed, you may choose to contact DFAS to confirm that they received the trust and that all is in good order through any of their customer service avenues. If you feel you need additional assistance, you can also contact a special needs consultant at Military OneSource at 800-342-9647.

In summary, do the following if you want to list your child as a beneficiary under the SBP for your military pension:

- Your dependent child must be **properly listed** in DEERS as permanently disabled.

- You must establish a **first-party SNT** to receive the pension payments.
- You must submit the trust and relevant forms to **DFAS** so the pension can be directed to the trust.

Without this planning, your child may lose eligibility for Medicaid or SSI due to income thresholds. Some may think that the survivor benefits will be enough, but you should be sure to read through the financial planning sections of this text to help you determine what resources you need to address your loved one's cost of care.

COORDINATING MULTIPLE INCOME SOURCES

For some children from military families, the combination of a Medicaid waiver, the SBP from a military pension, TRICARE for Life, and SSI/SSDI-DAC provide enough resources to cover their cost of care and all of their daily living needs. These can create a solid foundation of lifetime support.

Families then have the flexibility to reserve assets in a trust or ABLE account to fund large purchases such as accessible vehicles, a down payment on a home, or life-enhancing therapies.

If the Medicaid waiver is not available due to location or waitlists, the military pension and TRICARE become even more critical to sustain long-term care.

WHO CAN HELP

There are many professionals, in the military and in the civilian world, who can help. For military-specific services, Judge Advocate General's Corp (JAG) Legal Services can help with reviewing legal documentation and SNT creation. Current service members and retirees can access JAG benefits by contacting their local JAG office or visiting its website.

The Exceptional Family Member Program (EFMP) has coordinators available to connect families with services. Coordinators can provide information, referrals, systems navigation, and nonmedical case management. The EFMP program is only available for current service members—not retirees.

DFAS representatives are another wonderful source of information. They can be reached many different ways and can provide guidance on submissions, trust documentations, SBPs, and more.

And of course, special needs financial planners are a great way to start. We encourage you to check—are they familiar with military planning? You want to make sure you are working with a team or firm that is familiar with military planning and SBP options.

This may seem like a ton of people and coordination—that's because it is! The good news is, many people and professionals are ready and able to help and guide you through the process—to make sure that your family and your loved one have the best possible outcome.

A couple of important notes: a surviving spouse cannot disclaim their benefit. Once the SBP has been elected, the spouse must claim and receive the SBP before the dependent child can claim the benefit. Additionally, the election to pay the benefit to the SNT is irrevocable, meaning, it cannot be changed. You want to be certain this is your choice, as there are no takebacks.

FINAL THOUGHTS

Military families can create a powerful support plan by coordinating the Survivor Benefit Pension, Social Security Disabled Adult Child benefit, Medicaid waiver services, and TRICARE for Life. Done correctly, this layered approach can provide medical care, housing support, and personal enrichment opportunities for a loved one with special needs.

It is an extraordinary way to continue serving—by ensuring your child is protected, supported, and respected for the rest of their life.

Chapter 16

Education, Section 504, IEPs, and Your Child

As parents and caregivers, we spend considerable time supporting our loved one's education. Whether it's helping your child to get special education services, or advocating for an accommodation in the classroom, or finding support for social skills and friendships, schooling can be hard to navigate. Schools not only provide a path to graduation and ultimate employment opportunities, but they provide access to recreational and social opportunities, driver's education, vocational training, and so much more. Education has evolved over the decades and can now be provided in various ways including traditional public-school programs, private schools, online academies, residential schools, homeschooling, and various hybrid systems. Educational programs and services can be quite innovative and, depending on where you live, can offer unique and alternative approaches to meeting educational requirements.

In the United States, education is compulsory, typically from the ages of 6–16, although it varies from state to state. It is a state's responsibility to regulate education requirements and degree pathways, in accordance with federal regulations. What is offered in each state can differ significantly with some states offering an easier pathway for charter schools and others offering public specialty programs for high school students, as some examples. It will be important to take time to understand what is offered in your state and what might be the best fit for you and your loved one.

For students with disabilities, schooling has historically been a challenge. Most people with disabilities were excluded from education until the Education for All Handicapped Children Act of 1975, which has now evolved into the current law, IDEA (Individuals with Disabilities Education Act). Before that time, schooling was often not welcoming or supportive of students with disabilities. In many cases, students with disabilities were not expected to make progress, in contrast to their nondisabled peers. It is hard to believe how long it took for the national schooling system to permit students with disabilities to attend school and then the years it took since that time to set the expectation that students with disabilities can and will learn. The years it took for students with disabilities to get the support and recognition they deserve set a tone that to this day families are still trying to overcome.

The special education process set forth in IDEA and the Section 504 accommodations are in place in public schooling to protect and support students with disabilities. This chapter addresses the needs of students with disabilities including how to understand Special Education, IEPs and Section 504 Plans, and the advocacy process for students with disabilities.

According to the National Center for Education Statistics, the 2022/23 school year reported that the number of students aged 3–21 who received special education and/or related services under IDEA was 7.5 million, or the equivalent of 15% of all public-school students, with the most common disability category being specific learning disabilities. That number is significant.

IDEA presently is a law that makes available a free, appropriate, public education (FAPE) to eligible students that ensures special education and related services to those students. More specifically, the four parts of IDEA include (1) the general provisions of the IDEA law, (2) services for children aged 3 through 21, or until their graduation from high school, (3) services for infants and toddlers, birth to age 3, qualifying them for free, family-focused services, and (4) an outline of grants and funding for programs that help students with disabilities get a better education.

The foundational principle of IDEA is FAPE. IDEA requires that FAPE be provided in the Least Restrictive Environment (LRE) to the maximum extent possible, which creates a responsibility for schools to serve students in the general education environment, with inclusion and access to grade-level learning whenever possible. LRE provides that students with disabilities have meaningful access to same aged peers without disabilities, when appropriate. Access to the general education curriculum and classroom can be provided in several ways including using adapted curriculum, providing additional adult support, using assistive technology, or in other ways as determined by the special education team in collaboration with the family and student.

> **NOTE:** IDEA stands for the Individual with Disabilities Act, FAPE stands for a Free and Appropriate Public Education, and LRE is the Least Restrictive Environment. These acronyms are used often when talking about special education in public schools.

Taken together, FAPE and LRE are considered in decisions about a student with disabilities and their needs. This could apply in a situation, for example, in which a neighborhood school is unable to provide needed services and programming to guarantee FAPE within the general education classroom. In that instance, the school district would be responsible for working through the IEP process to design an individualized program and placement that meets the student's needs. In that situation, the school district may find that a program in a different neighborhood may have the needed services and work with the family to support the student's participation in that program, rather than the one in their own neighborhood. Although that seems less than ideal, the focus in the IDEA regulation and process is to consider the student's needs and to put together a plan that supports them in consideration of FAPE and LRE.

UNDERSTANDING IEPs AND 504s

Again, the eligibility process can take different forms, but the main focus of it is to make sure students that meet requirements are identified while those that don't are not misidentified. School districts may use the same process to evaluate students under IDEA and Section 504; however, they must be sure to adhere to IDEA requirements or the regulations of Section 504. It will be important to understand the process at your local public school system when it comes to eligibility. The eligibility process can include school specialists conducting assessments, interviewing family members, classroom observations, and any other information that will help the eligibility team in their determination of eligibility.

The Difference Between an IEP and a 504 Plan

An IEP and 504 Plan differ in many ways, but they also share some similarities. They are both founded on FAPE, both require an eligibility process, and are both legally binding. Their differences, however, include the following:

- **Eligibility Process:** A student may be found eligible for an IEP if they have 1 of the 13 disability categories in IDEA and require special education or related services to make progress in school. A student can be identified as disabled and may receive the protections of Section 504 and classroom accommodations, even if they do not qualify for special education under IDEA. Sometimes students who do not qualify for an IEP may receive a 504 Plan; this is not always the case but could occur if it was determined to be the best way to address the student's needs.
- **Funding:** IDEA provides for some funding grants toward the provision of special education services. However, Section 504 provides no financial support to school systems.
- **Intent:** The 504 Plan ensures a student receives the necessary accommodations to access the general education curriculum while removing barriers by providing testing accommodations, curriculum, or classroom accommodations. An IEP may also have accommodations, but it also has specific interventions and services.

The eligibility determination process identifies which is appropriate for the student. That process of determination consists of the school conducting and reviewing assessment information, hearing concerns, and coming together as a team, with you included, to understand and address the needs of your loved one. Since the school team is directed to conduct testing and to administer the eligibility process, often as a family member you are "outnumbered" in the process. This part can feel stressful. It can also feel overwhelming to know your child needs help while having to go through a process that feels like you must prove that they need and deserve services.

A Look Inside IEP and 504 Plans

Special education and school based disability services are focused on helping a student to access the curriculum, school, environment, and learning. These services are wide ranging and can include help from specialists like behavior analysts, speech therapists, and counselors as well as supports such as modifications, social skills groups, and interventions. Be sure to check your state and local guidance documents to understand the processes available to you and your child. An IEP consists of measurable, annual goals for the student as well as a list or description of the special education, related services, supplemental aids, and services that the school will provide.

It also contains the present level of academic performance—meaning a measure of how the student is currently doing—so that progress can also be measured. This looks like a statement that describes the student's present levels of academic achievement and functional performance and how the student's disability affects their involvement and progress in the general education curriculum.

There will be annual, and measurable, goals. If you feel your IEP is vague and the goals are not quantified and measurable, you have the right to go back and ask for a meeting to review these and make changes. Several of those goals will focus on academic and functional skills that correspond with measures of progress to be monitored.

The IEP will also detail what services are being provided, from special education, therapies, and supplementary aids and services. Details include any services and supports provided by the school and is often described in terms of hours and frequency. Any accommodations (which are distinctively different from services, aids, and therapies, as mentioned previously) are also detailed. An example of an accommodation would be allowing a student to take a test in a room by themselves or to have extra time on a test or quiz.

You will also find testing, graduation, school personnel, and other details relevant to the person with a disability. The format of the IEP can vary so be sure to check with your local special education director to learn what to expect in your child's school.

A 504 Plan lists the accommodations the student with a disability needs. These can include supports such as preferential seating, extra time on tests, using speech-to-text for writing, modified textbooks, adjusted class schedules, services, and other supports based on the individual needs of the student as well as the findings of the evaluation or eligibility process. The 504 Plan normally lists the accommodations as well as the staff who will oversee ensuring adherence to it.

THE IMPORTANCE OF COLLABORATION

If you are feeling overwhelmed or concerned about the eligibility or special education process, here are some pointers to keep in mind. First, collaboration is key. You *are* part of the team, even if there is one of you sitting across the table from many school professionals. It is important to build a collaborative mindset from the beginning. The eligibility and special education processes are dedicated to your child and the more you focus attention on that, the better. Get to know your team members. Be sure there is time at every meeting to introduce yourself, give an update, and share pictures and information about your child. It is even better if your child can attend meetings with you, if they are comfortable with that and if you feel it is appropriate. Meetings with the school can feel overly formal, it helps to keep in mind that the formality is there for a reason, to ensure a fair process that addresses your loved one's needs. If you can take time to connect with your school team, to build rapport, and to keep your loved one front and center, it should help to make you more comfortable.

It is also important to take time to prepare. Read your Notice of Procedural Safeguards, which the school will provide to you, and read all drafts and documents that are sent to you. Take time to review testing information before the meeting. If the school team does not provide this information to you before the meeting, you need to reschedule as they should be sending you information ahead of the meeting, per the procedural safeguards. You are entitled to time to review content and to understand the information. It is okay to ask questions; try to make a list before your meeting so that you are sure to address what is on your mind.

Because there are so many pieces that go into schooling supports, we also recommend working with an advocate or a parent with experience in this process to support you. There are paid advocates and public advocates, based on where you are located. Alternatively, talk with an experienced parent and ask them to join you as you go through the eligibility process. You always have the right to bring an advocate and to seek guidance throughout the special education process.

CASE STUDY: THE BRIMMON FAMILY

Ian is a second-grade student attending his local public school. During kindergarten and first grade, Ian had a number of challenges such as difficulty with attention, poor peer interactions, and he found it a struggle to participate in group activities. Ian's mom, Cara, often talked with the teacher to strategize his issues and at one point she started working with the school counselor each week to get additional support with his behavioral challenges.

But now that Ian is in second grade, his challenges have intensified. On the second day of school, the teacher called and asked Cara if Ian had ever been evaluated for disabilities. By the end of the call, Cara and the teacher had agreed to schedule an initial eligibility hearing. Fast forward, several weeks later, the school was moving through the eligibility process to determine whether Ian qualified for accommodations and/or special education. Since this was Cara's first time in the process, she asked one of her neighbors for advice. Her neighbor, Michele, had a child with autism, and Cara knew she had been through a similar process. Michele offered to join Cara at the meetings and to help walk her through the details. Cara was relieved. Although the school was being very kind and helpful, the whole process felt intimidating.

Cara was not familiar with the assessments they were doing and didn't know what she needed to ask for or how to navigate the resources. She was completely overwhelmed. Having Michele by her side was comforting, and Michele was able to point out a few items that the school had not included that needed to be addressed.

Whether you are like Cara and just starting out or like Michele and mentoring others on their path, the education system is complex. There are numerous regulations on top of school codes of conduct and requirements. It is hard to find the time to take in the information and understand what your next steps are. And, on top of that, it is such an important process. The schools provide access to specialized support and services, the very things our loved ones need. We must make time to take in the information and participate fully in determining what our loved one needs and how to get it.

ADVOCACY IN THE EDUCATION SYSTEM

From preschool through high school—and sometimes beyond—advocacy in education is critical. Most families engaged with the IEP process report feeling underprepared. For example, you should know that you have the right to request evaluations at any time. From the beginning, when you believe your child might have the need for an IEP, to the time where an IEP is in force but you feel not fully addressing their needs, a parent can request an evaluation from the school. Be sure to read and review your Procedural Safeguards; they support your right to address issues you find with the special education process.

Every state's guidance document will explain the guidelines and contacts around special education and supports in your area. There are specific IDEA processes, timelines, and documents such as prior written notice, meeting requests, consent, and so much more. We could write an entire book on school supports and advocacy, but instead and for the sake of time, we are focusing on the advocacy side of services, which are often the hardest part for a family to navigate. And if you feel you are not making progress with the school, are not being listened to, or simply need support, remember that you can always bring an advocate or a trusted person to meetings. Unfortunately, many IEP meetings can feel confrontational. As parents who are also advocates, we walk a fine line of creating a team that wants to go the extra mile for our child, while also knowing our rights and making sure our child is getting the supports and education they are entitled to receive.

Schools and districts have their own role to play here. We have attended IEP meetings as advocates where the school has more people in the meeting representing the school on a legal basis than there are people who know or have worked with the child. This can be very intimidating to parents. Some parents will hire their own attorney or professional advocate. Still others will bring a trusted relative, friend, or fellow parent to be a second set of eyes and ears. Not only will it allow you to not be gaslit, it will also provide you with someone who can be less emotional and allow you to fill the parent role while someone else acts more as an advocate. We have been there—we know that when the school is trying to intimidate, we can lose our train of thought or not ask all the questions we had prepared.

No matter what path you take, knowing what is available to your child through IDEA and their right to FAPE is necessary. We recommend you take a look at the legislation in its entirety—and if you want more information, call your local Parent Education and Advocacy Chapter—each state has them, although they are called different things in different states.

You should also know that you can pause, reschedule, or disagree with the school's recommendations. One family called us and said that an IEP meeting had been held without them because the school was not able to accommodate their schedule. One day they were called and asked to pick up their son from school due to what they deemed misbehavior. As they picked him up, his aid brought out the IEP and demanded their immediate signature, stating he would no longer be eligible for IEP services unless they signed immediately.

Not only did they not sign, but they asked for what was their right—an IEP meeting that showed his Behavior Intervention

Plan, the data they had collected, and why it was not working, causing him to be picked up by mom and dad on a regular basis. After several more months of the school showing they were unable to implement the Behavior Intervention Plan, collect appropriate data, and provide the supports needed for their son, the school agreed to fund a publicly funded, private day placement.

One of the keys to the family's success was how much documentation they kept of the process. Every meeting, email, conversation was written down and/or recorded. When a conversation was had verbally, an email recap was sent. Key decision-makers were kept in the loop. No one was able to pretend they were not aware of the situation. In the end, the parents' advocacy and team they put together resulted in the best outcome for their son: placement in a school that truly fit his needs, paid for by the school that did not have the resources to support their child.

That example illustrates an important point: if it's not in writing, it didn't happen. Document everything. Email recaps of conversations and keep meeting notes.

For more information about IEPs and you and your child's rights, we encourage you to check out the US Department of Education's Parent Guide to the IEP: https://sites/ed/gov/idea/parents. At the time this book is being written, the Department of Education is being disbanded. It looks like IDEA enforcement and IEPs will be housed under Health and Human Services. Links may no longer work, and we will do our best to post updated links and citations on our website for parents and families.

We have found that in the IEP process, there are certain common issues that families encounter. The first is obvious: outright denial of services. But denial of services may not always be cut and dry. It may be a school denying a child access to a field trip or isolating a child from their peers that may otherwise thrive in a social environment with peers. It could also be about physical accessibility: not having wheelchair access to the science lab, for example.

Gaps in communication are also common. Not keeping parents in the loop about assessment results or not updating the IEP in a timely manner are two common ones. Pushing timelines out due to lack of staffing is another. States usually set their own guidelines for communication and timing of communication. Knowing those guidelines—finding them on your state's department of education website—will help you know how to advocate for your child.

The bottom line is that your child's experience in school will benefit from your close collaboration with the school team. It is important to work together. However, it is also important to express what you need to express, to ask questions, to share your concerns, and to question decisions. You can be the advocate your child needs by participating in the process.

It is important to keep your child front and center at all meetings. Sometimes when we ask questions, we worry that we will hurt the teacher's feelings or cause people to think we don't appreciate what they are doing to help our child. But we can have both. We can appreciate the help while still serving as our child's advocate. Again, take someone with you who can help shoulder some of the discomfort often felt during the process and to partner with you as you navigate the process.

CONSIDERATIONS FOR STUDENTS OUTSIDE OF SPECIAL EDUCATION

So far we've discussed the regulations and requirements within special education and how to navigate those processes. But many students with disabilities do not receive special education services or 504 plans. Some students with learning disabilities, ADHD, anxiety, health issues, or other conditions do not need special education services.

This exclusion can be because their diagnosis does not limit their access to the environment and their ability to learn, or it can occur when a student pursues special education but does not meet the eligibility requirements. Some students take medication that helps support them throughout the school day, potentially reducing or eliminating their need for services or supports.

Other students may use outside supports and services through therapies or in-home supports after school, which meets their needs. In other cases, students attend private, nonpublic schools, home schools, or online programs that do not offer special education services. If a nonpublic school option is best for your student, please keep in mind that they may not have ready access to the supports often found in public school or publicly funded programs (a publicly funded program describes a state-approved and state or public funded private day or alternative option).

Another important consideration for students enrolled in nonpublic school options is that they may not have access to the special education or eligibility processes inherent in those systems. For example, the eligibility process can identify a disability and that documentation that they established during the eligibility process can be valuable in the future when that same individual is preparing for a Social Security determination process.

Similarly, an IEP that documents a disability and the supports and services in place at the school might aid a Medicaid waiver or Social Security application in adulthood. And vocational services that are often provided in public schools starting around age 14 in most states can provide valuable assessment information and documentation for future benefits applications.

The most important thing to know about having a child with a disability outside of the public school system is that your child does not fall under the IDEA legislation and a private school is not subject to FAPE and LRE. This is different than a student who is sent to a private school because the public school does not have the resources and so the public school system is paying for their tuition. The public school still follows that student and is responsible for ensuring the child is subject to FAPE and LRE. If a parent (outside of the public school system) enrolls their child in a private school, microschool, or homeschool, they are declining the protections of IDEA and thus FAPE and LRE.

This means the private school can expel them for any reason and is not subject to enrolling your student either. You may find that there is a private school you trust that is known for accommodating students with disabilities; however, we want you to be aware of the risks and lack of protections.

If you choose to not participate in the public school system eligibility processes, it may mean that while your child is under the age of 18, you may need to seek out private evaluations to document their disability and the support needs and services associated with it.

Some parents who enroll their child with a disability in a private school have missed out on the free, detailed assessments used in school that automatically document the child's disability and services. If you are in this situation, be sure to think about what documentation you have and what you might need, if you need to consider adult disability benefits.

START YOUR BINDER: GET EVERYTHING IN ONE PLACE

As you put together your family's special needs plan, we recommend creating a binder. One section of that binder should be Advocacy and include evaluation reports, correspondence with the school, and goals and data tracking forms. Having one section for each chapter of this book will help your family keep track of important documents, thoughts, and information you will need for your special needs plan.

We cannot emphasize enough that keeping good records will be an important key to your success. Kristin's son is five years old, and she has been told she may not need to provide his brain scan to Social Security until he is 18. Yet they may need it—even though it was done when he was only a day old. In a world where we are told to ruthlessly declutter, make sure you are hanging onto these important documents—they may serve more than one purpose and could be helpful for future benefits evaluations when you must prove onset of disability happened before a certain age.

FINAL THOUGHTS

Schooling is challenging at times, but keep in mind that your child has a right to education. The special education system as well as the availability of private, alternative options are designed to address diverse learning needs. We suggest taking intentional time to learn what is available to you where you live and to identify a person who can join you in your journey advocating for your loved one.

Chapter 17

Special Needs Planning and Grandparents

In our experience, special needs planning is multigenerational. Grandparents are often involved, especially when children are young and need more support, while parents are juggling multiple priorities—therapies, medical appointments, careers and providing financially for their family, and more. Grandparents are able to fulfill a special role in supporting their children and grandchildren when disability impacts the next generation.

We approached one of our favorite grandparents, John Bryan, to tell us about his approach to special needs planning for his autistic granddaughter. John Bryan is a successful author in his own right, having written *Angelina's Shake-A-Stick*, and founded the Autism Grandparent's Club, which continues to provide community and advice to autism grandparents on the journey today.

HOW I APPROACHED SPECIAL NEEDS PLANNING

By John Bryan, Autism Grandparent

All of a sudden ...

On June 29, 1983, JC and I received a telephone call that we had thought might never come: we were going to have a baby. But not in six months or seven months or eight months—we would have a baby in just nine days! We had thought that our long adoption search would go on forever; the phone call was an unexpected, wonderful surprise.

Only nine days to plan for a baby. Our first child. No crib, no diapers, no bottles, no experience. So, I quickly shared the news with my neighbor who had two young children: "Great news! We're going to adopt a baby in nine days! Can you make me a list of what we need?" My neighbor just smiled and shook his head. All of a sudden, without the normal multi-month notice, we were confronted with the many aspects and challenges involved with planning for a baby.

Fast forward to 2016. Kelly, our 1983 surprise baby, was in the hospital assigned to bed rest for what was categorized as a "high risk" pregnancy. Angelina, our first grandchild, was born at 25½ weeks, weighed 1½ pounds, and spent 130 days in the NICU tethered to wires and tubes while undergoing all sorts of surgeries and other invasive procedures. We spent all of our time and energies focused not on planning for Angelina's future, but on her survival.

Angelina survived. She is almost nine years old as I write this. She no longer has any physical disabilities, and most persons who don't have much familiarity with autism wouldn't recognize that she is on the spectrum. And today all of us in her family have a level of comfort and experience with "special needs planning." But it took a lot of time and energy.

Although JC and I were jolted back in 1983 by the sudden, unexpected need for baby planning, our family was much more jolted and ignorant and inexperienced regarding the sudden need for special needs planning. And, as every special needs family knows, special needs planning is far more complicated and wide-reaching and challenging than planning for a typical baby. We quickly recognized a factor that has been extremely helpful from the beginning: grandparents often have time and resources and energy and experience that—because of what are often 24/7 challenges—are not easily available to special needs parents.

Where to start ...

As Angelina neared her first birthday, I suspected autism: no eye contact, no smiles, no babbling, etc. When she came home from the hospital she had started speech therapy, occupational therapy, and physical therapy. None of her therapists ever said the word "autism" or used the phrase "special needs." Later I learned that therapists are cautious about using such terms.

I realized that it was probably time to start getting advice regarding how to put in place plans for a special needs child. And I suspect that most special needs families—just as it was with us when we got that phone call back in 1983 and later with Angelina—don't have a lot of advance notice.

What to do first? I contacted and met with two persons who were extremely knowledgeable and experienced: a long-time autism mom who had been a special needs pioneer and professional in my community, and a longtime autism grandfather who had conceived and built our community's, and now one of the nation's, best autism service facilities. My question was the same for both: "Where do we start?" Their advice for first steps: get an official diagnosis and then start ABA therapy. Which we did. Angelina was diagnosed as autistic, and we enrolled her in ABA.

Of course, at the time we didn't know anything about how an autism diagnosis works or what ABA is; we simply trusted the guidance of two persons with longtime experience and expertise. My advice for other brand-new special needs families regarding where to start? Get advice from the most experienced and credentialed persons in your community. If you don't know who they might be, your local school system and your local special needs nonprofit organizations should be able to point you to the right persons.

Apart from Angelina's health and development, my thoughts quickly went to money. How much money will be needed for Angelina's lifetime? Internet research on the websites of reputable autism organizations all had the same answer: as much as possible. Angelina's parents don't have a lot of expendable income or a legacy bank account, so my first steps were to talk with a trusted financial advisor and an attorney who was experienced with special needs. Those conversations resulted in a special needs trust which will generate funds to help Angelina throughout her adulthood—a larger amount of money than we thought might be possible.

After engaging Angelina in appropriate therapies, including ABA, and putting in place an initial financial plan, our seemingly overwhelming task was to put together a comprehensive and multifaceted plan—and to first identify the elements of such plan. In our case it is important to note that JC and I have a great relationship with Angelina's parents, and thus they were, and continue to be, happy with our willingness to conduct online research, talk with professionals, attend meetings, etc. This enabled us to contribute a lot of legwork to the planning process—legwork that special needs parents often don't have time for.

Next steps ...

Fortunately, there are companies that specialize in not only expertise and legwork for special needs families but can also provide ongoing coordination and oversight. We were fortunate to have two friends, both special needs parents as well as experienced professionals, who together had recently formed such a company. And early on we engaged in what they said was a mutually beneficial arrangement: they provided us with their services in exchange for our feedback and suggestions. I like to think this was as helpful to them as it was for us.

Another important factor is that JC and I spent, and continue to spend, a lot of time with Angelina. So, we had, and continue to have, first-hand knowledge of just about everything about her—thus allowing us to provide first-person information and observation to Angelina's therapists, healthcare workers, teachers, etc., as requested and needed.

We quickly realized that there was important day-to-day information concerning Angelina that needed some sort of organized repository—a repository that could accommodate continual changes. So, we put together a looseleaf notebook and labeled it, "ANGELINA NOTEBOOK." We modified it as things changed. The notebook had seven sections. "CONTACTS" contained the list of persons whom we might need to contact at any given time: Angelina's physicians, therapists, ABA company, Kelly's work and school information, etc. "EMERGENCY MEDICAL INFO" contained the things, including insurance info, that healthcare workers would need to know if there were ever an emergency. "FOOD" was a continually modified list of things that Angelina was able to eat/drink. (It is common for autistic children to have eating challenges.) "ROUTINE MAINTENANCE" was a continually decreasing list of healthcare-related duties: g-tube, nasal cannula, medicines, etc.—all of which finally disappeared. "FUN STUFF" was a continually changing list of things that Angelina liked to do. "VIDEOS" was an evolving list of things that Angelina greatly enjoyed watching on television. (I still love *Maya the Bee*.) And finally, "GOALS" was a list of short-term aspirations such as sitting up for a full minute without toppling over, enunciating certain letters of the alphabet, etc.

The expansive plan ...

Getting a handle on a fully comprehensive long-term planning process was a much bigger challenge. Plus, it came with the understanding that publicly funded services are continually subject to legislation that results in modification and even cancellation. It is rare that a special needs family has the time or expertise to keep up with everything needed to put in place and maintain a comprehensive plan, so it is essential to get ongoing consultation from experts. Which our family did and does.

We decided to develop a "Life Plan" notebook for Angelina. And we got, and continue to get, expert advice from professionals, respected websites, and experienced autism families. On one website I found a video discussion entitled, "Almost Everything I Know About Autism, I Learned from Other Parents!" Special needs parents are great sources of practical information: how to navigate the waiting lists are for certain services, where to find healthcare specialists, which therapists are best, and on and on. And special needs parents, because they have actual frontline experience as opposed to professional knowledge, have been both victims and beneficiaries of things that can be known only through direct, in-person experience—such as learning that there is much more to an IEP meeting than what is in the guidelines.

Following are some of the sections of Angelina's Life Plan:

- **Money:** What are the sources and amounts of money that may be needed to assist and support Angelina? Special Needs Trust? ABLE (Achieving a Better Life Experience) account? What are potential sources of money? Will Angelina have the ability to earn money? A financial advisor can help.
- **Legal Concerns:** What will happen if/when Angelina's parents are no longer able to care for her? Should there be a plan for guardianship and/or power of attorney, and when might this happen? A special needs attorney can help.
- **Public Benefits:** What are the current and future sources of public support and benefits for Angelina? When are the appropriate times to apply? How do you keep up with the changes that continually happen with public support? Local social service agencies can help.
- **Decision-making:** When Angelina reaches adulthood, will she be capable of making her own decisions? If not, will she have a legal guardian who can make good decisions? If she *is* capable, should there be a person or group of persons who are willing to help her?
- **Health:** What are the details of Angelina's current physical and neurological health, including various therapies? What health concerns can be reasonably expected for the future? What parts of her health history are important to document? Who are the professionals who currently treat her health concerns, and what is the plan for transitioning to other professionals as needed in the future?

- **Abilities/Challenges:** What are Angelina's best current abilities and what are her significant challenges? What are reasonable expectations for the future? How is she currently dealing with challenges and what is the plan for the future?
- **Daily Routine:** What is Angelina's school/activity situation and what are the plans for her future—including when she is no longer eligible for publicly supported school? Is she a candidate for post-secondary education, and if so, what is the plan? Is she a candidate for getting a job, and if so, what is the plan?
- **Goals:** What are the top few goals for Angelina, and what are steps for reaching those goals? For example, one goal might be to develop some close lifelong friends.
- **Life Transitions:** What will be Angelina's significant transitions? (Adolescence, changing schools, ending schooling, changing homes, death of family members, illnesses, etc.) How can her family/friends continually help her prepare for them and make them as easy as possible?
- **Living Arrangements:** Where will Angelina live during the different phases of her life? (With her parents, independently, a group setting, assisted living, etc.) Are there ways to plan and prepare?
- **Interests and Socialization:** What things does Angelina enjoy doing with others? Are there additional social activities that she might enjoy, and what can be done to initiate those involvements? Are there things that interest her when she is by herself? What can be done to nurture activities that can become lifetime enjoyments?
- **Love of Friends/Family:** What can be done to assure that Angelina is always surrounded by persons who care about her? Is there an opportunity to nurture special friendships with much younger relatives and friends? Are there groups or organizations—such as faith-based organizations—that can provide her with a

sense of family? And if so, when and how should that involvement begin and be nurtured?
- **The Village:** Who are candidates to be members of Angelina's "Life Team"—persons who are willing to receive updates about her, willing to be called on for special favors and advice and support, and willing to confirm that Angelina is someone whom they care about and want to always be willing to help.

And finally ...

There are additional thoughts about the process of developing a Life Plan for Angelina. First, she should be personally involved in developing and continually modifying the Plan. That might mean asking her opinion about various aspects, and/or simply explaining things as they develop. Second, her Life Plan should be subject to ongoing modification as needed, and a total review at least yearly. Third, the maxim, "Hope for the best, but plan for the worst," should be in mind with every aspect of the Plan. And whenever we get a chance, we should seek advice from persons who are parents of special needs adults and ask for their thoughts on what components and strategies can be helpful.

And finally, it can be extremely helpful for special needs caregivers to engage with support groups. Not only does this allow for therapeutic commiseration, but it also provides information that can be invaluable for special needs planning. When JC and I became autism grandparents, there was no grandparent group in our community. (There is now!) So, we joined a national support group for autism grandparents and have benefitted from its grandparent-to-grandparent-to-grandparent Zoom meetings. Engaging with other special needs families can be very helpful for special needs planning.

FINAL THOUGHTS

All special needs families are different, and each family—as JC and I have learned—must blaze its own customized path for special needs planning. Would we do anything differently if given the chance to start over? Maybe move even more quickly with everything that needs to be learned and accomplished. It's never too early to start special needs planning, and you can never move too quickly to learn and do everything.

Chapter 18

Sibling Supports

When a family has more than one child with special needs—or when there is a mix of neurotypical and neurodivergent siblings—the planning process becomes layered with complexity. Each child may have different diagnoses, abilities, and needs. One may require full-time care, another may be semi-independent, and another may have no disability at all. Every family must balance fairness with functionality.

This chapter addresses how families can plan for multiple children with special needs, especially when needs are unequal. It explains how you can make decisions about dividing financial and caregiving responsibilities. You may need to establish fair expectations for typically developing siblings and to prevent conflict and preserve sibling relationships into adulthood. And how to support siblings who will play a role in long-term care of their disabled sibling.

We know that this is a similar chapter to the estate planning chapter that discusses the "equitable but not equal" distribution of assets. As it is a topic that comes up again and again, we thought it worth delving into in more detail.

CASE STUDY: THE PARKERS

The Parker family includes two sons and a daughter: Ben, Theo, and Rosemary. Ben is 26 and has Down syndrome. He attends a day program and lives with his parents. Theo is 23 and has autism but independently navigates much of his day and has held a series of part-time jobs. Rosemary is 21 and is just finishing her final year of undergraduate school at the local university. Ben requires lifelong support and is already receiving Medicaid waiver services and DAC benefits.

Theo has never qualified for a waiver because he does not have an intellectual disability, yet he struggles with executive functioning and anxiety. He also relies on his parents for housing and daily routines. Rosemary has lived near campus in an apartment for the last year and intends to stay there after she graduates. She is only 25 minutes from home and makes time to visit with her family regularly most weekends.

The Parkers have had to ask difficult questions: Do they divide their estate equally? How can they ensure that Theo, despite being fairly independent, doesn't fall through the cracks? And what role will Rosemary play once they are no longer here? And, more importantly, how do they make sure Ben and Theo's care does not fall completely on Rosemary?

The Parkers work with a special needs financial planner to assign resources intentionally: a combination of special needs trusts, life insurance proceeds, and trust protectors for both sons—but tailored differently based on each need. A paid care manager and microboard have been added to ensure oversight. The microboard serves two purposes, to help navigate and advocate for resources while also supporting Rosemary by providing guidance and assistance.

These issues are real. As parents and caregivers, we worry about our disabled children and what will happen when we are no longer here. We also worry about other family members who don't realize the time and effort it takes to support the disabled members. We want to make sure everyone is happy and supported. This is an important goal—and it can be realized.

Too often families assume that their financial planning and legal documents are enough to protect and support their disabled children's lifetimes. However, we know that advocacy is actually the key ingredient. It is possible to establish pathways of advocacy ahead of time that work to support every member of your family. This is where sibling support comes in. Supporting siblings through equitable planning, advocacy, and intentional training makes a lasting difference.

This chapter shares how to support siblings through equitable estate planning, advocacy, and training. The first step is to identify what makes sense for your family.

WHAT THE FAMILY NEEDS TO FIGURE OUT

When you spend some intentional time with a framework established ahead of time, you will have a much higher chance of success in addressing common mistakes and planning gone wrong.

When support needs vary widely, take some intentional time to write down the needs of each child. If you have already put together a care plan for each child, get those out and start to look at how each child could be cared for. Would they be able to live in the same place? Will they need to live in different places, with different levels of support? What are your primary goals for them? What are *their* primary goals?

At this point in the book, you should also have their cost of care available. Have their individual cost of care available as you examine your estate and consider how to divide your assets. Look at what each member needs. The chapters on public benefits, financial planning, and estate planning provide detailed information on how to think through equitable distributions.

Now think through what your expectations are of your neurotypical child (if you have one). Make sure you have discussed with them in depth what your expectations are and train them on the details when necessary. Having conversations early and often can be the key to avoiding future resentments. While many parents are afraid to have these conversations, they are surprised when they do that the sibling is relieved—aware of the unspoken expectation and more afraid of the unknown and lack of support than they are of the expectation itself. You can't know this if you don't talk about it. And if they are not open to the caregiving, you will want to know that too, so that you can start to make alternate plans.

You will also want to think through the other things that can get in the way (even unintentionally) of a sibling providing support and care. A spouse may not be supportive. They may have disabled children of their own or have the opportunity for a dream job in a state where their sibling would not be eligible for a Medicaid waiver. Being prepared for these risks is very important, and providing your neurotypical child with a way to express their concerns and feel validated is also important.

Next think through, are you creating a structure to support them (e.g., microboard, care manager)? Think about yourself and how you've spent the lifetime of your loved one getting to know their needs, becoming an expert in their diagnosis, and following a complex care routine. It may not be enough to just have another person, even the sibling, step into that role alone. They haven't gone through or learned what you have. Even when sharing a household, a sibling may not have contact or interactions with the therapists, reports, case managers, and other processes, at the level you do. We can't assume that having them jump into our role will be enough or allow support to continue the way it has. Rather, we need to think about what resources the sibling will need to provide support.

And finally, think about your trustee and beneficiary designations. Do you need to revisit your trustee or beneficiary designations to avoid conflict? If a sibling is both a beneficiary and a trustee, this could pose conflict. The best way to address this is to talk with your attorney about the best options and to consider additional avenues of advocacy. Pairing a trustee with a microboard or embedding trust protectors can help ensure both support and appropriate decision-making.

WHAT IS EQUITABLE ESTATE PLANNING?

Equitable estate planning is a process of ensuring that your estate plan is fair by considering everyone's unique needs and circumstances rather than simply dividing an estate into equal shares. Sometimes parents worry that if they don't divide their estate into equal shares, their children may feel slighted, igniting family tensions and grief. However, with careful, intentional planning that is communicated in advance to every member of the family, these risks can be mitigated. Having conversations that explain the disabled member's needs, tools, and services and how you plan to address them is helpful, not harmful. Again, often siblings feel that they are "on deck," yet they aren't sure how everything is going to play out. Working through this together as a family is critical. As parents and caregivers of children with disabilities, the good old days of a surprise, magical inheritance are over. Instead, we must plan deliberately with a focus on protecting benefits, establishing long-term care, and supporting independence. This means we must be clear and careful about our process and craft a plan that makes sense for everyone and that is lasting.

Taking time to evaluate the needs of every member of your family is an important first step. The information you gather will help you determine how best to support your disabled family member(s) and their siblings.

CASE STUDY: THE JOHNSONS

When the Johnsons had their first child, Emma, she was diagnosed with a rare neurological condition requiring 24/7 care. Years later, their second child, Ava, was born. Ava grew up knowing her parents expected her to stay close to home and one day take over Emma's care. But Ava went away to college, started a career in another state, and married someone whose job moved them frequently.

The Johnsons hadn't developed a backup plan. There was no care manager, no microboard, and no system of professional support. When Emma's needs escalated and her parents aged, they faced crisis. Ava was overwhelmed, conflicted, and unprepared. The family needed a system, not just good intentions.

When Ava did what she thought was best and moved Emma to live with her, she had no idea what Medicaid or Medicaid waivers were. She had no care plan or idea of what Emma's daily routines were. Emma was thrown into further crisis, and Ava's own family felt thrown into crisis as well. Emma followed them around from state to state several times, before the family finally moved back to their hometown and were able to find a group home where Emma could live with some friends. It was a grueling and painful process for all, and one that more intentional planning and open conversation could have prevented.

HOW TO ESTABLISH A PATHWAY OF ADVOCACY

As parents and caregivers, we often figure out advocacy the hard way—by pulling resources together, finding supports, and managing the day-to-day routine. We learn as we go, working to understand everything we can about our loved one while simultaneously trying to do everything we can. And life goes on this way until before we know it, we are here wondering what will happen when we are no longer able to do so. Instead of focusing solely on who will step into our shoes, we need to think about the advocacy we now instinctively provide will carry on. There are several ways to do this.

We have outlined in previous chapters tools that can work together to make this all work. From a care plan, to a microboard, and an estate plan that goes beyond just documents to intentional communication and training, you have an idea of what the tools are. Now you need to knit them together in an intentional way that makes sense for your family.

We have met and supported countless siblings. And the resounding message we get from them is this: they want to help but they aren't sure they know how. Be sure to take time to create a pathway for siblings. Amanda Lukof is one sibling who takes support to the next level!

> **NOTE:** Intentional communication with your more typical children will help prevent headaches and resentment later!

CASE STUDY: AMANDA LUKOF AND ELEPLAN

Amanda Lukof is the founder of Eleplan, a company dedicated to providing the technological framework to house care plans, medical records, legal documents, and more—centralizing vital information into an easy-to-access system for families. Amanda's brother has autism and will need lifelong support. Rather than resenting her brother, Amanda has embraced him. She takes him on trips, makes sure he never misses a new episode of *Saturday Night Live*, and even met her husband through a fundraiser the family held to support her brother.

Amanda's husband understands and supports her ongoing role in her brother's life, and their children have a strong relationship with their uncle. When Amanda shared her story with a room full of parents and caregivers, there wasn't a dry eye. She emphasized that instead of resentment, her experience of growing up with a sibling with special needs has led to greater compassion, deeper purpose, and immense admiration for her mother. Her story reminds us: even when you feel like you're doing everything wrong, your children may be growing into thoughtful, resilient, and deeply empathetic adults.

As you put the pieces together, keep in mind that every effort goes nowhere if those around you aren't made aware. We must be intentional. It is not enough to just have the "stuff," you must take time to share and explain the information, answer questions, and guide those around you so that when you are less able to provide support, they can step in.

INTENTIONALLY INFORMING AND TRAINING OTHERS

This is by far one of the most missed steps! Take time to share what you have done with others. Whether you have multiple children with disabilities and have separate plans and documents for each and/or have neurotypical siblings, they need to know your plan. And we don't mean know that it is in a vault at the bank or in a shoebox under the bed. No, that won't work at all. We mean that you set aside time to meet with them and orient them to the supports outlined earlier. Once you have the initial meeting, we suggest scheduling an update meeting at least annually to check in, update the Care Plan, and make sure what you have still makes sense. Be sure to follow these steps:

- Identify who is on the team.
  - This step is about making sure we share the plan with those that need to be informed. This includes people listed in your estate plan, family members, possibly friends, and supporters. The individuals will be specific to your situation and needs so take time to identify who you need to address.

- Identify what they need to know.
  - Once you know the people, decide what they need to know. It could be that everyone needs to know the Care Plan. But maybe not everyone needs to know your financial plan or estate plan. It really depends. Decide who needs to know what and address them accordingly.
- Identify where this information will be stored.
  - This is so important. Where will you keep all this information? How will those that need the information access it? How are they informed of updates? Be sure to think through all these pieces so that not only do you have the information and the people identified, but the information remains accessible.

And last but not least, be sure to avoid pitfalls and common mistakes.

COMMON PITFALLS

Don't disinherit your special needs child! Even if your other child has the best intentions, anything could happen: divorce, premature death, bankruptcy, or their own disability. Along those lines, avoid naming a sibling as both trustee and remainder beneficiary. It creates a conflict of interest. Without clear guidelines, that sibling might limit spending from the trust to preserve the inheritance.

Make sure your expectations are explicit. If you want your typical child to take on a role, talk about it. Include them in planning. Make sure they're up to the task—and supported to do so.

And have a backup plan. Even a willing sibling may become unable to help—from sickness or disability of their own, a challenging family situation, or a failed business. A microboard, care manager, and professional trustee can help build resilience and intentional backups.

There is a lot of information out there. We hear misconceptions all the time. It is so important to surround yourself with experts who can guide you according to regulations and best practices. And, more importantly, make sure the professionals you use are experts in special needs planning. This type of planning is not a side gig or a one-off; it is highly specialized. A lot of misconceptions come from professionals who have expertise, but not in special needs planning. Be careful!

And as you move forth planning support for every member of your family, keep in mind that siblings supports can evolve. As each child grows, their goals and needs change. It will be important to include flexibility in your plan and to make adjustments as needed. The following case study illustrates this.

CASE STUDY: THE ROSAS

The Rosas family has two daughters: Lily, 29, and Marisol, 27. Marisol has a rare genetic disorder that limits her ability to live independently. Lily, though neurotypical, grew up deeply affected by her sister's needs—and inspired by them. She became a licensed clinical social worker specializing in emotional regulation and coping strategies for children with autism.

The family designed a plan where Lily is a member of Marisol's microboard but not her sole caregiver or trustee. A professional trustee and a trust protector help manage the finances. Lily lives in another city but remains actively involved, with monthly check-ins and a shared care app. She knows her sister has an inconsistent work history and hasn't been eligible for a Medicaid waiver, but the family has used a combination of private funds and ABLE contributions to support Marisol. For Lily, the experience of siblinghood has shaped her life's work—and with clear structures in place, she can support her sister without sacrificing her own goals.

FINAL THOUGHTS

Equity in planning means doing what's right for each child, not simply dividing assets equally. With thought, structure, and the right tools, families can preserve relationships and ensure that all siblings—disabled or typical—have the clarity, security, and support they need to thrive.

We know that some professionals will recommend hard and fast rules with siblings. We want you to know that you know your family best—and if you find yourself at an impasse, engaging professional support can help you guide your decision. However, do not make a decision that does not feel right simply because a professional recommended that path. You are the captain of the ship, and you direct your family's future. Professionals can help see blind spots you might not be aware of and help prevent future problems, but they do not know what is in your heart and that of your family. Move forward with purpose and love. Your family will be okay.

Conclusion: The First Step Is Yours

If you've made it to this point in the book, we want to say thank you. Thank you for taking the time to learn, to plan, and to think about the future of your loved one—and your whole family. This journey isn't easy, but you don't have to walk it alone.

At All Needs Planning, we believe that special needs planning is more than just legal documents and financial accounts. It's a deeply personal, family-centered process grounded in love, intention, and trust. We hope this book has given you a framework to begin—or continue—building a future that honors your loved one's dignity, supports their autonomy, and ensures their safety and well-being for years to come.

We also want you to know that we're here for you. If you're wondering what to do next, here are a few ways to stay connected. If you feel that you still need more education, we invite you to join the All Needs Learning Lab, an educational membership designed to help you understand in-depth the different parts of special needs planning. With videos and a social component, we aim to provide community and education—and regularly update content. You can learn more at allneedslearninglab.com.

If you feel that you have enough education and are ready to take the leap to seek advice, we encourage you to schedule a consultation with us. The process will start with Mary McDirmid, and if you decide to work with us, you will be able to work with every member of our team. We are parents, and we are professionals, and we get it. You can schedule with Mary at https://calendly.com/marymcdirmid/allneeds.

There are many other ways that you can engage with us as well.

- **Join our Facebook Group:** *Special Needs Planning with the All Needs Community*—a place for families to connect, share resources, and find encouragement.
- **Follow us on social media:** We post updates, articles, and planning insights regularly on **Facebook**, **Instagram**, and **LinkedIn**.
- **Visit our website:** www.allneedsplanning.com to learn more about our services, upcoming webinars, and scheduling options.
- **Attend a webinar:** We regularly host free planning sessions that break down the most important topics—trusts, guardianship, Medicaid waivers, financial strategies, and more. Once a year, we host a virtual special needs planning conference—focusing on the tools, strategies, and knowledge you need to be successful. We invite other professionals to bring in-depth knowledge to families, caregivers, and professionals.

This is a journey, and while the road ahead may sometimes feel overwhelming, you're not starting from scratch—you're starting from strength.

And remember: while some of the specifics discussed in this book may change—state Medicaid waiver availability, IRS guidance, or tax policy—the core principles stay the same. A good plan considers the **whole family**, draws from **every available resource**, and is built on **layered supports** that promote autonomy while safeguarding health, dignity, and choice.

It's never too early—or too late—to take that first step. We're ready when you are.

We are in this together,

Kristin, Kathy, and Mary
All Needs Planning

Notes

CHAPTER 1

1. Stat10. (n.d.). *1 in 10 Americans have rare disease, but few have treatments* [online]. Available from: https://www.statnews.com/sponsor/2022/10/12/1-in-10-americans-have-a-rare-disease-but-few-have-treatments/
2. US Center for Disease Control and Prevention. (2024). *Children and youth with special healthcare needs in emergencies* [online]. Available from: https://www.cdc.gov/children-and-school-preparedness/special-healthcare-needs/index.html
3. Jajtner, K.M., Mitra, S., Fountain, C., and Nichols, A. (2021). Rising income inequality through a disability lens: Trends in the United States 1981–2018. *Social Indicators Research*, 151(1): pp. 81–114. doi: 10.1007/s11205-020-02379-8

CHAPTER 2

1. Medicaid. (n.d.). *Home & community-based services 1915(c)* [online]. Medicaid.gov. Available from: https://www.medicaid.gov/medicaid/home-community-based-services/home-community-based-services-authorities/home-community-based-services-1915c/index.html
2. Internal Revenue Service. (2025). *ABLE accounts—Tax benefit for people with disabilities* [online]. IRS.gov. Available from: https://www.irs.gov/government-entities/federal-state-local-governments/able-accounts-tax-benefit-for-people-with-disabilities

3. Family Caregiver Alliance. (2016). *Caregiver statistics: Demographics* [online]. Available from: https://www.caregiver.org/resource/caregiver-statistics-demographics/

CHAPTER 3

1. *New York State Association For Retarded Children, Inc. et al. v. Hugh L. Carey*, 393 F. Supp. 715 (1975).

CHAPTER 5

1. Virginia Medicaid. (2025). *Developmental disabilities waiver services & rates* [online]. Available from: https://www.dmas.virginia.gov/media/uxipsn0c/my-life-my-community-rate-file-updated-7-26-2024a.pdf
2. Defense Finance and Accounting Service. (2025). *Special needs trusts (SNT)* [online]. Available from: https://www.dfas.mil/RetiredMilitary/provide/sbp/special-needs-trust/
3. Administration for Community Living. (2020). *How much care will you need?* [online]. Available from: https://acl.gov/ltc/basic-needs/how-much-care-will-you-need

CHAPTER 6

1. The Center for Medicaid and Medicare Services published an article on the history and current status of Home and Community Based Services waivers, written by Mary Jean Duckett, M.S.P., and Mary R. Guy, M.S. Ed., M.S.W.: https://www.cms.gov/sites/default/files/repo-new/50/00Fallpg123.pdf

CHAPTER 11

1. United Nations. (2006). *Convention on the rights of persons with disabilities* [online]. Available from: https://www.un.org/disabilities/documents/convention/convoptprot-e.pdf
2. National Council on Disability. (2018). *Beyond guardianship: Toward alternatives that promote greater self-determination* [online]. Available from: https://www.ncd.gov/assets/uploads/reports/2018/ncd_beyond_guardianship.pdf
3. National Resource Center for Supported Decision-making. http://www.supporteddecisionmaking.org
4. American Bar Association. (2023). *Supported decision-making* [online]. Available from: https://www.americanbar.org/groups/law_aging/publications/bifocal/vol_36/issue_5_june2015/supported-decision-making/
5. Social Security Administration. (2024). *Representative payee program* [online]. Available from: https://www.ssa.gov/payee/
6. National Guardianship Association. (2021). *State-by-state guide to guardianship and rights retention* [online]. Available from: https://www.guardianship.org

CHAPTER 12

1. Siegel, J. (2022). *Stocks for the long run.* 6th ed. New York: McGraw Hill Education.

CHAPTER 15

1. TRICARE for Life. https://tricare.mil/tfl
2. Defense Finance and Accounting Service. (2025). *Secondary dependency—Incapacitated child (21 years of age or over)* [online]. Available from: https://www.dfas.mil/MilitaryMembers/SecondaryDependency/SDC/Secondary-Dependency-Incapacitated-Child/

3. Miliary OneSource. (2024). *How to use the high-3 and final pay military retirement calculators* [online]. Military OneSource. Available from: https://www.militaryonesource.mil/financial-legal/personal-finance/military-retirement-calculators/
4. Defense Finance and Accounting Service. (2023). *Estimate your retirement pay* [online]. Available from: https://www.dfas.mil/retiredmilitary/plan/estimate/
5. Form available from: https://www.dfas.mil/Portals/98/Documents/About%20DFAS/Special%20Needs%20Trust%20Certification-%20For%20Attorneys%20Corrected%2020250905.pdf?ver=f0ly8or5-cnNCa62YgHs7A%3d%3d
6. Defense Finance and Accounting Service. (2025). *Welcome to ask DFAS* [online]. Available from: https://www.dfas.mil/dfas/AskDFAS/

Acknowledgments

This book could not have been written without the help of some key people in our lives. First off, special thank you to Judith Newlin at Wiley, who took a chance on us as previously unpublished authors and allowed us to put our expertise out into the world. Your feedback every step of the way, even when it was not part of your "job" per se, was invaluable and helped us get to the final product. We had no understanding of the publishing world, and you guided us through what to expect with patience and perseverance and gave a cursory read through our initial chapters as well. Special thanks as well to Venkatraman Sankar, our managing editor, who took our manuscript through the production stages, provided us with our key milestones, and held our hand to make sure everyone was happy with the finished product.

We want to thank our family and friends, who supported us as we wrote this book. Kristin wants to especially thank her husband Dave, who put aside every Tuesday night for her to work on writing—even though he was dubious of the end result. Kathy would like to thank her parents, Don and Bonnie Meincke, for cheering her on in every way, lifting her spirits, and reminding her of the important role family plays in every aspect of life.

Thank you to our guest contributors, John Bryan as an autism grandparent who was willing to share his personal perspective as well as his professional expertise, and Penelope Gaffney and Randi Johnson from Gravis Law. Your personal and professional expertise will provide different perspectives to our readers that are needed as they embark on their planning journey.

And lastly, thanks to our friends, clients, and families in the disability community. The Virginia Board for People with Disabilities has been an incredible source of information and connection, with a special call-out to Dr. Penni Sweetenburg, who leads Partners in Policymaking and helped bring a curriculum of advocacy, supports, and how to navigate a complex system with empathy to a group that included Kristin. Kelly Piacenti has been an incredible sponsor to us, providing guidance, feedback, and support at every step of our journey. Mary Morris and Walter Stosch in Virginia have been incredible personal supports and advocates to the disability community.

Thank you for your sponsorship, knowledge, and advocacy for the special needs community.

We are profoundly grateful to everyone who brought us here.

About the Authors

Kristin lives with her husband and two kids in Richmond, Virginia. A Blue Devil alum, she cheers passionately for Duke basketball (which her husband not so quietly tolerates). She enjoys hiking, skiing, and watching her kids try new things (and them laughing at her while she tries new things). Kristin has worked in finance for more than 20 years and began special needs planning when her son was born with agenesis of the corpus callossum, a rare brain disorder.

Dr. Kathy Matthews lives in Powhatan, Virginia, with her two boys and her two dogs. She enjoys spending time with her boys and extended family, being active, and listening to live music. Kathy has worked as professional administrator of the Faison Center for Autism, special education teacher, and licensed behavior analyst, and now enjoys extending her knowledge to advocate for families. Her professional life came full circle to her personal life when she realized her eldest son also had autism.

About the Authors

Mary McDirmid lives in Spokane, Washington, with her husband and two girls. She enjoys swimming, basketball, and the occasional triathlon—staying active is at the top of her priority list. Authenticity and being true to her inner self are Mary's top priorities—and she brings that every day to her work with special needs families.

Index

Note: Page numbers in *italics* and **bold** refers to figures and tables respectively.

A

ABLE accounts, 78–81
adults/supportive voices, 30
advocacy
    building sustainable
        advocacy, 24–25
    disability rights
        advocacy, 25–27
    embedding advocacy, 38–40
    IEP meetings, 24
    person-centered
        planning, 32–38
    self-advocacy, 27–31
    sibling supports, 277–279
Affordable Care Act, 103
"aha" moment, 3
The Americans with Disabilities
    Act (ADA), 25, 38
applicable multi-beneficiary
    trusts (AMBTS), 119,
    121–123
augmentative and alternative
    communication (AAC)
    device, 29

B

Bill of Rights Act, 26

C

Caregiver Alliance, 20, *20*
care plan
    behavior, 51
    capture what you
        know, 49–50
    case study, 42–43
    creation, 43–45
    describing supports, 52–53
    good care plan, 44
    joy, interests, and
        identity, 53–54
    overview, 41–42
    robust care plan, 44
    start small, 49
    step-by-step care
        plan, **55–60**
    supported adults, 45–48, *48*
    transitions, 52
    triggers, 51
    unthinkable happens, 54

Centers for Medicare & Medicaid Services (CMS), 97
Cobell v. Norton, 172
Convention on the Rights of Persons with Disabilities (CRPD), 175
convertible term life insurance, 132
counselors and therapists, 207
COVID-19 pandemic, 228

D

Defense Enrollment Eligibility Reporting System (DEERS), 232
Defense Finance and Accounting Service (DFAS), 74, 232
Developmental Disabilities Assistance, 26
developmental disability, 3
disability insurance
  long-term disability, 144
  own-occupation rider, 144
  short-term disability, 144
disability rights
  advocacy, 25–27
disabled adult child (DAC), 75, 232
  benefits, 16, 109
  case study, 112–113
  eligibility checklist, 110
  Medicare eligibility, 113–114
  SSDI-DAC benefit, 111
  SSI interact, 111–112
dollar cost averaging, 198–200
Down syndrome, 2

E

Economic Security Act, 97
The Education for All Handicapped Children Act (EAHCA), 25
Employer Identification Number (EIN), 127
equitable planning
  addressing future conflict, 159
  case study, 276–277
  child with disabilities, 157
  communication, 156–157
  legal considerations, 169–170
  Medicaid/supplemental security income (SSI), 156
  minor children and siblings, 168–169
  sibling involvement and expectations, 158
  special needs trust (SNT), 156
estate planning and strategies
  advanced medical directive documents, 151–152
  case study, 148
  common mistakes, 154–155
  definition, 148
  equitable planning, 155–159
  getting documents, 152
  power of attorney (POA) document, 151
  property and assets distributed, 153–154
  special needs trusts, 150–151
  trusts, 149
  wills, 149

The Exceptional Family Member Program (EFMP), 242
extended period of eligibility (EPE), 114

F

family and disability community, 40
Family Caregiver Alliance, 20
family-led advocacy, 27
Federal Benefit Rate (FBR), 108
fiduciary accountability, 172
financial planning
  ABLE accounts, 64
  caregiver needs care, 88, 91–92
  case study, 65–66
  cost of care, 67–69
  multigenerational, 87
  optimizing tools, 81–87
  overview, 63–65
  retirement planning, 69–81
  special needs families, 88
  special needs trusts, 85–87
  timeline for, **89–90**
  toolbox for special needs, **83–84**
  two-generation approach, 93–94
free, appropriate, public education (FAPE), 38, 247, 248
Full Retirement Age (FRA), 76

G

government benefit
  case study, 116–117
  with confidence, 115–117
  Medicaid waiver, 98–103
  overview, 95–96
  safety net, 96–98
  Social Security programs, 106–115
  traditional Medicaid, 103–105
  work incentive programs, 114–115
group term life insurance, 132
growth vs. dividend investing, 195

H

hard-earned retirement savings, 141
Hobbs ex rel. Hobbs v. Zenderman, 169, 172
Home and Community-Based Services (HCBS) waiver, 25, 99

I

IEPs and 504s plan
  advocacy in education system, 254–257
  annual and measurable goals, 250–251
  binder creation, 260
  case study, 253–254
  collaboration, 251–252
  eligibility process, 249
  funding, 249
  intent, 249
  overview, 245–248
  procedural safeguards, 252
  students of special education, 257–259

impairment related work expenses (IRWE), 106, 115
income investing
  case study, 190–191, 200–201
  dividend-paying companies, 201
  dividend reinvestment, 198–200, *199*, *200*
  dividends matter, 191–195
  dollar cost averaging, 198–200
  emotional investing, 197–198
  growth vs. dividend investing, 195
  overview, 189–190
  reliable income, 202
  sequence of returns risk, 196–197
Individualized Education Program (IEP) meetings, 24
Individuals with Disabilities in Education Act (IDEA legislation), 38, 246–248
insurance
  case study, 137–140
  convertible term, 135–137
  cost of care, 134–135
  disability insurance, 144–145
  family framework, 145–146
  irrevocable life insurance trust (ILIT), 141–142
  life insurance, 132–135
  long-term care insurance, 142–144
  purchasing insurance, **139**
  survivorship policy, 140–141
irrevocable life insurance trust (ILIT), 141–142
IRS Publication 590-B, 125

J

Judge Advocate General's Corp (JAG) Legal Services, 241

L

Lewis v. Alexander, 172
long-term care insurance, 142–144

M

Medicaid waiver
  advocacy, 100–102
  case study, 102–103
  caseworkers, 209
  cost snapshot, 39, *39*
  funding, 25
  government benefit programs, 98–103
  SSI eligibility, 101
  vs. traditional Medicaid, **105**
military families
  benefits, 233–234
  case study, 232
  cost of living adjustments (COLA), 237
  DEERS registration, 231, 234–237
  DFAS, 233
  help, 241–242

multiple income sources, 241
pension analysis, 237–241
TRICARE for life, 231, 232, 234–237
MyChart, 2

N

National Foundation for Special Needs Integrity v. Reese, 170, 172
Neonatal Intensive Care Unit (NICU), 6

O

Office of Civil Rights, 23
Olmstead v. L.C., 26
own tax ID, 128

P

personal advocacy, 102
person-centered planning
  federal funding, 35
  IDEA legislation, 38
  legacy of self-determination, 33–34
  policy advocacy, 35
  public services, 34
  self-advocacy, 37
policy advocacy, 35
power of attorney (POA), 179–180
Presumed Maximum Value (PMV), 108
Primary Insurance Amount (PIA), 76

procedural safeguards, 252
Program Operating Manual System (POMS), 108
Protection and Advocacy system, 26
publicly funded programs, 258

R

Ramey v. Rizzuto, 170, 172
relax and enjoy
  budget creation, 228–229
  case study, 218, 224–225
  community programs, 228
  guidelines, 219–221
  movement and exercise, 226–228
  practical tools, 221–224
  travel destinations, 225–226
required minimum distributions (RMDs), 123, 126
retirement planning
  ABLE accounts, 78–81
  DAC benefits, 75
  Health Savings Accounts (HSAs), 77–78
  pensions and survivor benefits, 73–74
  retirement accounts, 71–73
  Social Security benefits, 75–76
Roth conversion
  case study, 124–125
  checklist, 125–126
  required minimum distributions (RMDs), 123, 126

S

Sabrina's SSI benefit, 131
Secure Act, 86
self-advocacy
  adults/supportive voices, 30
  communication, 29
  definition, 27
  legal planning, 32
  modeling, 29
  person-centered planning, 28
  rights and responsibilities, 31
  supported decision-making process, 29, 30
  teaching, 28, 31
self-care
  case study, 214–215
  find your people, 212
  identify your needs and goals, 212
  invisible toll, 204–209
  respite, 213–214
  schedule and execute, 212
  self-care, 210–211
  special needs children, 211
  stress levels, 211
separate tax ID, 128
sibling supports, 271–272
  addressing common mistakes, 273
  advocacy, 277–279
  case study, 272–273
  common pitfalls, 280–282
  equitable estate planning, 275–277
  informing and training others, 277–279
  unspoken expectation, 274
Social Security Act, 96, 99
Social Security Disability Insurance (SSDI), 109
Social Security Number (SSN), 127
Social Security programs
  business arrangement, SSI, 108–109
  SNAP benefits, 106
  SSDI-DAC benefit, 109
  SSI appointment, 107
special needs planning
  abilities/challenges, 268
  ABLE account, 17
  caregiver alliance, 20, *20*
  case study, 10–12
  DAC benefit, 16
  daily routine, 268
  day-to-day supports and decisions, 12–19
  decision-making, 267
  goals, 268
  grandparents, 261–270
  grow phase, 19
  health, 267
  interests and socialization, 268
  journeys, 1–7
  legal concerns, 267
  life transitions, 268
  living arrangements, 268
  love of friends/family, 268–269
  money, 267
  overview, 9–10
  protect portion, 17–19

Index **301**

public benefits, 267
Social Security benefits, 14
special needs trust (SNT)
  anticipating transition points, 167–168
  care committee, 164
  case study, 10–12, 165–171
  emotional impact, 170–171
  equitable planning, 156
  first-party trust, 162
  legal precedents, 171–173
  Medicaid waiver programs, 161
  overview, 9–10
  pooled SNT, 163–164
  SECURE Act, 164–165
  self-settled trust, 162
  springing trust, 162
  stand-alone SNT, 162
  testamentary trust, 166–167
  third-party trusts, 162–163
  trust protector, 164
speech therapy, 29
SSI earned income exclusion, 115
Starbucks trips, 131
step-by-step care plan, **55–60**
students of special education, 257–259
Supplemental Security Income (SSI), 95
supported decision-making (SDM)
  benefits of, 178
  case study, 176–177, 181–182, 185–187
  conservatorship, 180–181
  guardianship, 180–181
  legally binding, 178
  medical directive, 179–180
  microboards, 183–185
  overview, 175–176
  power of attorney (POA), 179–180
  risk of inaction, 182
  support methods, 185, **186**
Survivor Benefit Plan (SBP) payments, 74
survivorship life insurance, 133, 141

T

tax flexibility and strategy, 119–120
  applicable multi-beneficiary trusts (AMBTS), 121–123
  estate plans, 120
  grantor trusts, 128–129
  missing tax guidance, 127
  nonprofit remainder beneficiary mishap, 126–127
  own tax ID, 128
  Roth conversion, 123–126
  Secure Act, 121
  separate tax ID, 128
  special needs trusts, 127–128
  stretch IRAS, 121
Temporary Assistance for Needy Families (TANF), 106
term life insurance, 132

testamentary trust, 166–167
traditional Medicaid, 103–105
trial work period (TWP), 114
TRICARE for Life, 231, 232, 234–237

U
universal life insurance, 133

W
whole life insurance, 132
Willowbrook Consent Judgment, 26
Willowbrook: The Last Disgrace, 27
work incentive programs, 114–115